WHO NEEDS SANTA

SHADOWS OF SHAME:
OVERCOMING TOXIC SHAMING & EMBRACING SELF-WORTH

S.Y. VIDAL

Copyright © 2024 by S.Y. VIDAL

All rights reserved. No part of this publication may be reproduced, distributed, or transmitted in any form or by any means, including photocopying, recording, or other electronic or mechanical methods, without the prior written permission of the publisher, except in the case of brief quotations embodied in critical reviews and certain other noncommercial uses permitted by copyright law.

Published by Rosemary Woodlands Publishing
San Juan, Puerto Rico USA
www.rosemarywoodlands.com
First Edition
ISBN: 979-8-9911231-1-2
Printed in the United States of America

This book is a work of non-fiction. Names, characters, places, and incidents are the product of the author's experience. Any resemblance to actual persons, living or dead, or actual events is intentional.

For the silent warriors battling their own shadows.

"Shame may cast long shadows, but it cannot extinguish your light. Embrace your truth, for in the face of darkness, your resilience shines brightest."

- S.Y. Vidal

CONTENTS

CHAPTER 1 - PG 7

AN INTRODUCTION TO THE SHADOW OF SHAME

CHAPTER 2 - PG 13

THE FAMILY TREE OF SHAME

CHAPTER 3 - PG 27

THE INTERGENERATIONAL ASPECT

CHAPTER 4 - PG 43

RECOGNIZING SHAME PATTERNS

CHAPTER 5 - PG 61

THE PATH TO HEALING

CHAPTER 6 - PG 75

BUILDING RESILIENCE

CHAPTER 7 - PG 85
RECLAIMING IDENTITY

CHAPTER 8 - PG 97
FOSTERING HEALTHY RELATIONSHIPS

CHAPTER 9 - PG 111
BREAKING THE CYCLE

CHAPTER 10 - PG 123
PRACTICAL EXERCISES & RESOURCES

PG 133
REFERENCES

CHAPTER 1
AN INTRODUCTION TO THE SHADOW OF SHAME

Picture this: You're standing in front of a funhouse mirror. You know, the kind that distorts your reflection, making you appear taller, shorter, wider, or wavier than you really are. Now imagine living your entire life in front of that mirror, believing that warped reflection is the real you. That, my friends, is what it's like to grow up with toxic shame.

Welcome back, dear readers. If you've picked up this book, chances are you've already joined me on the wild ride through my first literary rollercoaster, "Who Needs Santa? & Other Lessons in Surviving Toxic Parents." If not, don't worry—you're still in for one hell of a journey. Think of this as the sequel, but instead of battling the Empire, we're taking on an enemy that's a lot closer to home—the shame that toxic parents plant deep within us.

In our last adventure, we unpacked the baggage of growing up with a narcissistic mother who could give Joan Crawford a run for her money in the "Mommie Dearest" Olympics. We laughed, we cried, we probably wanted to throw the book across the room a few times (I hope you didn't—those things aren't cheap!). But through it all, we began to understand the complex tapestry of abuse and neglect that forms the backdrop of so many childhoods.

Now, we're diving deeper. We're going to explore the sticky, uncomfortable, often invisible residue that those toxic relationships leave behind—shame. Not the garden variety "I wish the earth would swallow me whole" embarrassment you feel when you call your teacher "Mom" (been there, done that, got the therapy bills). No, we're talking about toxic shame—the kind that seeps into your bones and convinces you that you're fundamentally flawed, unworthy, and unlovable.

But here's the thing—that shame? It's not yours to carry. It never was. It's a hand-me-down from parents who were likely carrying their own shame, passed down through generations like some sort of twisted family heirloom. And just like that ugly vase your great-aunt Mildred left you, it's time to decide whether you want to keep lugging it around or finally let it go.

In this chapter, we're going to shine a light on this shadow that's been following you around. We'll explore what toxic shame is, where it comes from, and why it's stickier than that gum you accidentally sat on in third grade (another stellar moment in my personal hall of fame).

So, buckle up, buttercup. This ride might get a little bumpy, but I promise you, the view at the end is worth it. Because once you understand shame, you can begin to see it for what it really is—not a reflection of your worth, but a distortion that's long overdue for shattering.

Are you ready to break some mirrors?

Let's dive in.

First, let's talk about what toxic shame really is. Toxic shame isn't just the occasional feeling of embarrassment or guilt we all experience. It's a pervasive sense of being fundamentally flawed and unworthy of love and belonging.

It's the dark cloud that hovers over your every move, casting a shadow of self-doubt and insecurity. Imagine waking up every morning with a voice in your head that says, "You're not good enough," "You're a failure," or "Nobody could ever truly love you." This is the reality of living with toxic shame.

Toxic shame is often planted in childhood, taking root through the words and actions of those who were supposed to nurture us. It's the criticism that stings like a slap, the punishment that feels more like retribution than discipline, and the affection that's withheld as a form of control. These experiences teach us to see ourselves as inherently flawed, and this belief becomes the lens through which we view the world.

For instance, let's consider how a parent's constant criticism can shape a child's self-perception. If you were repeatedly told, "You're too sensitive," or "Stop crying, you're being a baby," you might have learned to suppress your emotions, believing that your natural reactions were wrong. Over time, this suppression can lead to a disconnect from your true self, making it difficult to understand and express your own needs and feelings.

Another common source of toxic shame is the inconsistency in parental behavior. One moment, you're the golden child, praised for your achievements; the next, you're a disappointment for not living up to impossible standards. This emotional whiplash can make you feel like you're constantly walking on eggshells, never sure of your place or worth. It's like playing a game where the rules keep changing, and no matter how hard you try, you can never win.

Religion can also be a breeding ground for toxic shame, especially when used as a tool for control rather than a source of comfort. Growing up, I was dragged to church services multiple times a week, where the sermons were filled with fire-and-brimstone warnings about eternal damnation. It wasn't just about fearing divine retribution; it was about internalizing the belief that I was inherently sinful and unworthy of love.

These experiences don't just sting in the moment; they leave lasting scars. They shape the way you see yourself and the world around you. When you're told repeatedly that you're not good enough, that you're a disappointment, or that your true self is unacceptable, you start to believe it. The shame seeps into your bones, becoming a part of your identity.

But here's the good news: toxic shame can be unlearned. It takes time, effort, and a lot of self-compassion, but it's possible. The first step is to recognize the shame for what it is—a distortion, not a truth. It's about seeing the funhouse mirror for what it is and realizing that the warped reflection is not the real you.

In the coming chapters, we'll explore how to dismantle these distortions and reclaim your true self. We'll look at practical strategies for healing and building resilience, and we'll hear stories of others who have walked this path and come out stronger on the other side.

So, are you ready to shatter those mirrors and see yourself clearly? Let's dive deeper into the shadow of shame and begin the journey to healing and self-acceptance.

CHAPTER 2
THE FAMILY TREE OF SHAME

"The apple doesn't fall far from the tree," they say. But what if that tree is rooted in toxic soil, watered with criticism, and pruned with emotional neglect? Welcome to the orchard of intergenerational trauma, where shame isn't just a fruit – it's the whole fucking harvest. Picture a family reunion, but instead of potato salad and awkward small talk, everyone's passing around hefty servings of "you're not good enough" with a side of "why can't you be more like your cousin?" Sounds fun, right? About as fun as a root canal performed by Edward Scissorhands.

In this chapter, we're going to climb that gnarly family tree and take a good, hard look at how shame gets passed down from one generation to the next. It's like a game of Hot Potato, except the potato is on fire, covered in spikes, and nobody wants to admit they're playing. Remember how in the last chapter we talked about shame being a hand-me-down? Well, it's time to buckle up, because we're about to dive into the vintage shop of family dysfunction.

We'll explore how Grandma's inability to express love turned into Mom's constant criticism, which blossomed into your own feelings of never being "enough."

But here's the thing – understanding this cycle isn't about playing the blame game. It's not about pointing fingers at Great-Aunt Ethel and her penchant for backhanded compliments. It's about recognizing the pattern so we can finally say, "Thanks, but no thanks" to this family tradition.

Grab your emotional hard hat. We're about to do some excavating in the family archives. Don't worry if it gets a little dusty – I've packed tissues and a sense of humor. Trust me, we're going to need both.

Ready to shake that family tree and see what falls out?

Now that we've set the stage for our family reunion of shame, what exactly is this toxic shame we keep talking about, and how is it different from that guilt you feel when you eat the last slice of pizza without offering to share? (Not that I've ever done that. Ahem.)

Toxic shame is like wearing a pair of glasses that make everything look awful, especially yourself. Imagine waking up every day and putting on glasses that distort reality, turning every glance in the mirror into a harsh critique. It's not just feeling bad about something you've done; it's feeling that you, as a person, are fundamentally flawed or unworthy. Guilt says, "I made a mistake." Shame whispers, "I am a mistake." See the difference? One's about your actions, the other's about your very existence.

When you experience guilt, it's typically tied to a specific event or action. You forgot your friend's birthday, and you feel guilty about it. You skipped a workout, and you feel guilty for not sticking to your routine. Guilt can be a healthy emotion, prompting you to make amends and change your behavior. It's like a nudge from your conscience reminding you to align your actions with your values.

But shame? Shame is a whole different beast. It's not content with critiquing what you did; it goes straight for the jugular, attacking who you are. Shame takes those moments of guilt and magnifies them, distorting them into a narrative about your worth as a person. Forgetting your friend's birthday doesn't just make you feel bad; shame tells you that you're a terrible friend, that you're selfish and unlovable. Skipping a workout isn't just a lapse in discipline; shame insists that you're lazy and will never be good enough.

This insidious whisper of shame embeds itself into your identity, making it hard to see yourself clearly. It's like having a constant, negative voice in your head, always ready to tear you down. This voice doesn't just appear out of nowhere. It's often born out of critical or abusive environments where the message you received repeatedly was that you are not enough. Over time, these messages become internalized, and you start to believe them as truths about yourself.

The impact of living with toxic shame is profound. It affects your self-esteem, your relationships, and your ability to pursue your goals. When you believe that you are fundamentally flawed, it's hard to take risks or put yourself out there. Why try for that promotion if you're convinced you're not capable? Why enter a relationship if you believe you're unworthy of love? Toxic shame creates an invisible barrier, keeping you trapped in a cycle of self-doubt and self-sabotage.

Furthermore, shame often masquerades as other emotions, making it tricky to identify and address. It can show up as anger, lashing out at others because it feels safer than confronting your own vulnerabilities. It can appear as perfectionism, a desperate attempt to cover up perceived flaws by being flawless. It can even manifest as depression or anxiety, weighing you down with a sense of hopelessness and fear.

Breaking free from the grip of toxic shame requires more than just positive thinking or self-affirmations. It involves a deep, often challenging process of self-examination and healing. This journey starts with recognizing the difference between guilt and shame and understanding how they each play a role in your life. It's about learning to remove those distorted glasses and see yourself through a lens of compassion and truth.

Imagine what it would be like to wake up one day and see yourself clearly for the first time, to understand that you are not your mistakes, and that your worth is not defined by the harsh words of your past. This is the goal of healing from toxic shame—to reclaim your true self from the shadows of doubt and to step into a life where you are no longer bound by the fear of being unworthy. It's a journey worth taking, and it starts with acknowledging the power that shame has held over you and deciding to change the narrative.

In abusive environments, shame becomes the air you breathe. It's in every criticism, every punishment, every withheld affection. Imagine a garden where instead of nurturing the plants, the gardener constantly tells them they're growing wrong. Instead of sunlight and water, they get a steady stream of poison. That's what it's like to grow up in a shame-inducing household—your growth stunted, your spirit withering under the weight of constant negativity.

Your abusive parent might have said things like, "Why can't you ever get anything right?" or "You're such a disappointment." These aren't just harsh words; they're shame grenades, exploding all over your self-esteem. And just like real grenades, the damage isn't always immediately visible, but boy, does it leave scars.

Imagine being a kid, eager to share your latest accomplishment, only to be met with a dismissive sneer or a cutting remark. Instead of praise or encouragement, you get, "Is that the best you can do?" It's like trying to grow a flower in a toxic wasteland. Every attempt to thrive is met with a fresh dose of poison, ensuring that you never feel worthy of love or respect.

And then there are the subtle, insidious comments that linger in the back of your mind, gnawing away at your self-worth. I remember being told, "Why do you even try? You'll never be as good as anyone else." It wasn't just a blow to my confidence; it was a wrecking ball, smashing through any sense of self-esteem I had managed to build. These words weren't just criticisms—they were declarations of my supposed worthlessness, repeated until I started to believe them.

Think of shame as a parasitic vine, wrapping itself around your self-worth, squeezing the life out of it. In an abusive household, this vine is cultivated meticulously, with every snide remark, every comparison, every withheld bit of affection acting as fertilizer. Over time, the vine grows thicker and stronger, making it harder to see yourself clearly through its tangled mess.

When you grow up in an environment where shame is the norm, it becomes almost impossible to separate your true self from the distorted image your abuser has created. You start to believe that you are fundamentally flawed, that no matter what you do, you'll never be good enough. It's like trying to climb a ladder that never ends; every rung you reach is met with another insult, another put-down, pushing you further into the abyss of self-loathing.

And the effects of these shame grenades aren't just emotional—they're physical too. Chronic shame can lead to a host of issues, from anxiety and depression to eating disorders and self-harm. Your body literally carries the weight of your emotional wounds. It's like being in a constant state of fight-or-flight, with your nervous system perpetually on high alert, waiting for the next attack.

One vivid memory I have is of being criticized for something as trivial as the way I walked. "Why do you walk like that? You look ridiculous." It sounds absurd, but those words stuck with me. Every step I took felt scrutinized, and I became hyper-aware of my movements, always second-guessing myself. It wasn't just about walking; it was about the underlying message that everything I did was wrong, that I was inherently flawed.

Now, imagine being a queer kid in this environment. The scrutiny didn't stop at my walk. Anything that hinted at my true self was put under the family microscope and dissected like a high school biology project. I had to hide parts of myself, tucking away anything that might be seen as "girly" or out of the norm. It was like trying to stuff a rainbow into a plain brown box—impossible and suffocating. The church added another layer of shame and fear.

Growing up, I was forced to attend a Southern Baptist church every Sunday morning, Sunday night, and Wednesday night. Over the summer, there were Vacation Bible Schools and whatever else the church was up to. The indoctrination was relentless. One particularly scarring experience was a youth night at a deacon's house where they made us watch "Left Behind," an apocalyptic movie starring Kirk Cameron. It scared the literal shit out of me. Here I was, already grappling with my identity, and now I had to worry about being left behind when the rapture came because I was "sinful."

The church preached about homosexuality with the subtlety of a sledgehammer. According to them, all gays were destined to burn in a lake of fire for eternity. Imagine sitting through those sermons, knowing deep down that you were everything they condemned. It felt like being trapped in a horror movie where the monster was you. Each sermon added another layer of fear and shame, making me feel like I was inherently evil just for being myself.

One of the most hurtful experiences was when my grandmother, who had always been a source of comfort to me, sent me a handwritten letter condemning me to the fires of hell for posting a meme on Facebook. The meme showed an old couple holding a protest sign that read, "Your gay marriage doesn't affect our straight one." My grandmother's letter was filled with fire and brimstone, condemning me without a hint of the love she once showed. I never received an apology for that letter, and it stung deeply.

I vividly remember sitting with my grandmother in the church pew as a child. She would lovingly stroke my arm with her long nails, something that brought me immense comfort. One Sunday, she pointed to the pastor's son and his girlfriend sitting in front of us and whispered, "That will be you one day." The irony was rich, considering my ass was as gay as a Judy Garland tribute concert. Her words were meant to be encouraging, but they felt like a reminder of the lie I was living.

These experiences compounded the shame I already felt from my family. The toxic cocktail of religious dogma and familial expectations created an environment where I felt constantly judged and unworthy. It was like being in a never-ending performance where any misstep could lead to eternal damnation. The pressure to conform to their idea of a "good Christian boy" was overwhelming and isolating.

Religious shaming didn't just affect my self-esteem; it eroded my sense of identity. I became adept at hiding my true self, playing the role they expected, while secretly loathing the facade I had to maintain. It was exhausting and soul-crushing. The fear of being "found out" was a constant companion, making me hyper-vigilant about my behavior and appearance.

In these moments, I learned to find small rebellions where I could. Maybe it was sneaking a look at a fashion magazine, or enjoying a song that wasn't "appropriate." These small acts of defiance were my way of holding onto my true self, even if it was just for a moment. They were my lifeline in an ocean of shame.

The impact of these experiences is something I still carry with me. The wounds from those years of religious and familial shaming took a long time to heal, and some scars remain. But recognizing the roots of that shame has been a crucial step in my healing journey. It's about understanding that the shame I felt wasn't a reflection of who I am, but a product of the toxic environment I was in.

So, if you ever find yourself struggling with the weight of religious or familial shame, know that you're not alone. Many of us have walked that path, and there is hope on the other side. It's possible to reclaim your identity and find peace, even if it means unraveling the tightly wound threads of shame one by one. Remember, you are worthy of love and acceptance just as you are, no matter what anyone else says.

Witnessing my parents talk about the "girly" things I did that needed to be changed was a special kind of torture. My grandfather once bought me some troll baby dolls, the soft ones, for my birthday, and you'd have thought he brought home a ticking time bomb. The looks on my parents' faces were priceless—priceless in the sense that I wished I could pay to never see them again. The dolls disappeared faster than a piece of cake at a kid's party, and I was left with the unspoken rule: "Boys don't play with dolls."

These moments weren't just about curbing my behavior; they were about erasing parts of who I was. Every time I showed a hint of femininity, it was met with comments like, "Stop acting like a girl," or "That's not how boys behave." It wasn't just a slap on the wrist; it was a full-on assault on my identity. I learned to suppress my interests, hide my true self, and fit into the mold they demanded. The message was clear: being myself was unacceptable.

The impact of these experiences was profound. I started to police myself, hyper-aware of every gesture, every interest, every word. If I enjoyed a "girly" activity, I did it in secret, away from prying eyes. Watching cartoons or playing with toys that I actually liked felt like sneaking into a speakeasy during Prohibition—thrilling but laden with fear of being caught.

The fear of being "found out" extended beyond my family. At school, I was careful not to appear too different. I avoided activities that might draw unwanted attention or ridicule. I remember wanting to join the dance team but settling for something deemed more "appropriate" by societal standards. It was like living with a mask glued to my face, never able to let it slip, even for a moment.

This constant hiding took a toll on my mental health. The shame grenades thrown at me for simply being myself created deep-seated insecurities. I internalized the idea that my true self was something to be ashamed of, something to hide away. It wasn't just my family's disapproval I feared; it was the judgment of the world around me. I became a master at blending in, at playing the role of the "acceptable" boy, even though it felt like slowly dying inside.

Looking back, I can see how these experiences shaped my sense of self-worth. I wasn't just hiding my interests; I was hiding my identity. The constant message that I was wrong for being who I was left scars that took years to heal. The fear of rejection and ridicule made it hard to embrace my true self, even when I was finally in a place where I could.

Here's the thing—no matter how hard you try to bury your true self, it eventually finds a way to surface. It took time, courage, and a lot of unlearning, but I began to embrace the parts of myself that I had hidden for so long. I started to defuse the shame grenades, recognizing them for what they were—tools of control and suppression, not reflections of my worth.

If you ever find yourself walking in a way that feels right to you, even if it's not "approved" by others, keep walking. If you enjoy something that others deem inappropriate for your gender, keep enjoying it. The world is full of people trying to fit into molds that don't suit them, but life is too short for that kind of nonsense. Embrace your quirks, your interests, your true self. And remember, the only approval you really need is your own.

Now, let's talk about the long-term effects. First up, self-esteem. Toxic shame doesn't just dent your self-esteem; it takes a sledgehammer to it. You might find yourself constantly seeking approval, terrified of rejection, or believing you don't deserve good things. It's like having a gremlin on your shoulder, always whispering, "You're not good enough."

Imagine every time you muster the courage to take a step forward, that pesky gremlin leans in and says, "Remember, you're fundamentally flawed." It's like trying to drive a car with the parking brake on—no matter how hard you press the gas, you're always held back. This internalized shame manifests as a constant, gnawing self-doubt. Even when you achieve something, the gremlin is quick to remind you that it's probably a fluke, and any moment now, everyone will see you for the imposter you are.

This relentless whispering affects every aspect of your life. At work, you might hesitate to ask for a raise or promotion, convinced that you're not really worth it. You might overwork yourself, trying to prove your worth to your boss, only to burn out and feel even worse about yourself. It's the classic hamster wheel—running fast, getting nowhere.

In relationships, this gremlin can turn you into a people-pleaser. You agree to things you don't want to do, afraid that saying no will make people reject you. You might stay in unhealthy relationships because deep down, you believe you don't deserve better. The fear of being alone, combined with the belief that you're not worthy of love, keeps you trapped in cycles of dependency and dissatisfaction. It's like signing up for a lifetime of starring roles in a never-ending production of "Who's Afraid of the Big, Bad Rejection?"

Then there's the issue of self-sabotage. Toxic shame makes you your own worst enemy. You might procrastinate on important projects, avoid taking risks, or undermine your own efforts just as you're about to succeed. Why? Because success would contradict the narrative that you're unworthy. It's like that scene in every horror movie where the character is about to escape but trips over nothing—except in this case, you're tripping yourself on purpose.

Let's not forget the physical toll this takes. Chronic shame can lead to stress-related illnesses, such as anxiety, depression, and even autoimmune disorders. Your body becomes a battleground, constantly fighting a war against itself. It's like having an app running in the background of your mind, draining your battery life without you even realizing it.

For me, the gremlin showed up in the form of constant self-criticism. Every time I tried something new, it was there to remind me of past failures. "Why bother? You'll just mess it up like last time." It wasn't just about fear of failure; it was a deep-seated belief that I was fundamentally incapable of success. This gremlin didn't just sit on my shoulder; it moved in, rearranged the furniture, and set up camp.

Social situations were another minefield. Walking into a room full of people felt like navigating a gauntlet of judgment. I'd replay conversations in my head, dissecting every word, convinced that I had said something stupid or offensive. It was exhausting, like trying to win an argument with a hyper-critical inner monologue that never shut up. The impact on my self-worth was profound. I found it difficult to accept compliments, always suspecting that people were just being polite. Genuine praise felt like a setup, a prelude to the inevitable reveal that I was a fraud. It was like living in a constant state of impostor syndrome, where any moment, someone would rip off the mask and expose the "real" me—flawed, inadequate, and unlovable.

But here's the twist: recognizing the gremlin is the first step to evicting it. Understanding that these whispers of inadequacy are the echoes of past shame can help you start to challenge and change them. It's about rewiring your brain to see that you are deserving of good things, that your worth is not defined by the mistakes you've made or the harsh words of others.

One of the most powerful tools in this journey is self-compassion. Learning to treat yourself with the same kindness and understanding you would offer a friend can begin to dismantle the gremlin's hold. It's about catching yourself in those moments of self-criticism and asking,

"Would I say this to someone I care about?" If the answer is no, then it's time to reframe the thought.

Imagine transforming that gremlin into a supportive ally. Instead of whispering words of doubt, it reminds you of your strengths and achievements. It's not about becoming arrogant or delusional; it's about recognizing your true worth and potential. It's about giving yourself permission to succeed and to enjoy that success without guilt or fear. So, the next time the gremlin tries to whisper in your ear, remember: you're not obligated to listen. You have the power to change the narrative, to rewrite the script that has been handed to you. It's a process, and it takes time, but every step you take towards self-acceptance and self-love weakens the gremlin's grip. You are enough, just as you are, and no gremlin can take that away from you.

Ready to start unpacking that shame suitcase?

Let's do this!

CHAPTER 3
THE INTERGENERATIONAL ASPECT

Shame has a way of wrapping itself around family trees like an insidious vine, choking out the light and stunting growth. If you've ever wondered why certain negative patterns keep showing up in your family, the roots often run deeper than you might think. This chapter delves into how shame and toxic behaviors are passed down through generations and how cultural factors play a role in this perpetuation.

Imagine a dusty old attic filled with relics from the past. Among the boxes of forgotten memories and moth-eaten clothes, there's a trunk labeled "Family Shame." You didn't pack it, and you certainly didn't ask for it, but here it is—your inheritance. Unlike old photos or heirlooms, this trunk contains the weight of unspoken criticisms, unresolved traumas, and generational guilt. It's like inheriting your great-uncle's old toupee collection—you didn't want it, but now you're stuck figuring out what to do with it.

From the moment we're born, we start absorbing the emotional atmosphere around us. If your parents carried their own burdens of shame, it's likely they inadvertently passed some of it onto you. They might have done this through harsh words, unrealistic expectations, or even through their own self-critical behavior. Children are like emotional sponges, soaking up the unspoken cues and overt messages they receive. It's like marinating in a toxic sauce before you even realize you're the main dish.

Think back to your childhood. Did you often hear phrases like, "Why can't you be more like your brother?" or "You'll never amount to anything"? These aren't just offhand comments; they are seeds of shame, planted deep in your psyche. Your parents might not have intended to harm you, but their words and actions were shaped by their own experiences and the emotional legacies they inherited. It's like a family recipe for disaster, handed down through generations.

Parents are often products of their upbringing, carrying forward the lessons and wounds they received from their own parents. They might have faced harsh criticism or emotional neglect, and without realizing it, they pass these behaviors onto their children. It's a chain reaction, each generation adding another link to the cycle of shame. Picture it: Grandma's icy glares become Mom's scathing remarks, which then turn into your own inner critic's greatest hits album.

Let's consider an example. Suppose your mother grew up in a household where showing emotion was considered a weakness. Her parents might have dismissed her feelings, saying things like, "Stop crying, you're being ridiculous," or "Only babies get upset over something so small." She learned to suppress her feelings and put on a stoic front to gain approval and avoid ridicule. When she had you, she passed on that same belief, perhaps unintentionally shaming you for expressing vulnerability. Over time, you internalized the message that showing emotion is a sign of weakness, and thus, began the cycle of shame.

This pattern isn't limited to expressions of emotion. It can manifest in many areas of life. For instance, if your father was raised with the notion that financial success is the only measure of a person's worth, he might have pressured you to achieve and criticized you harshly for any perceived failures. His own fear of inadequacy and failure, instilled by his parents, becomes the lens through which he views and judges your accomplishments. Imagine living in a house where every C on a report card was met with the same reaction as if you'd set the backyard on fire. Fun times, right?

The emotional echoes of these inherited behaviors and attitudes create an environment where love feels conditional and self-worth is always in question. A parent who was never shown unconditional love may struggle to provide it, leading to a household where affection is doled out based on performance rather than as a constant, unwavering presence. It's like trying to grow a garden in a desert—you can water it all you want, but something fundamental is missing.

These emotional echoes can be more subtle. Perhaps your grandmother always kept a pristine house because she believed any sign of disorder was a personal failing. Your mother inherited this belief and instilled in you the idea that cleanliness equals worthiness. As a result, any mess in your home triggers feelings of inadequacy and shame. You're not just cleaning up the kitchen; you're scrubbing away layers of generational anxiety.

Unresolved trauma is another significant factor in the transmission of shame. If a parent has not addressed their own traumatic experiences, they may inadvertently project their pain onto their children. This can manifest as overprotectiveness, harsh discipline, or emotional unavailability. The child, in turn, internalizes these behaviors and carries them forward into their own relationships and parenting. It's like trying to outrun a shadow—it sticks with you until you turn around and face it.

For instance, if a parent experienced abuse in their childhood, they might overreact to normal childhood behaviors, seeing them as threats rather than natural developmental stages. Their hyper-vigilance and overreactions teach the child that the world is a dangerous place and that they must constantly be on guard. This perpetuates a cycle of fear and shame, where the child grows up feeling that they are always one step away from disaster. It's like living in a perpetual state of DEFCON 1, where every minor mishap feels like the end of the world.

Culture plays a significant role in how shame is transmitted and experienced. In some cultures, the family unit's honor and reputation are paramount, and any deviation from expected behavior can bring shame upon the entire family. This pressure to conform can be overwhelming, instilling a deep fear of failure and a persistent feeling of not being good enough. It's like living under a microscope, where every move is scrutinized and judged.

In contrast, other cultures might emphasize individual achievement and autonomy, which can also lead to shame when individuals feel they don't measure up to societal standards. The cultural context provides the backdrop against which family dynamics play out, shaping the ways in which shame is both inflicted and experienced. It's like trying to dance to a tune that keeps changing—no matter how hard you try, you're always out of step.

Imagine each family is a square in a vast cultural quilt. The patterns and colors of each square are influenced by historical events, societal norms, and collective values. Some squares are stitched with threads of resilience and support, while others are marred by expectations and judgments. The way shame is woven into your family's square of the quilt depends on the cultural threads available.

For instance, in many Asian cultures, the concept of "face" or honor is deeply ingrained. Bringing shame to oneself can be perceived as bringing shame to the entire family. This cultural backdrop can intensify feelings of personal inadequacy. Imagine living in a household where every action you take isn't just about you but a reflection on your entire lineage. It's like having a constant panel of judges rating your life decisions on a scale from "acceptable" to "ultimate disgrace."

In these cultures, academic and professional achievements are often seen as the pinnacle of success, leading to immense pressure on individuals to excel. A less-than-perfect performance in school or at work isn't just a personal setback; it's a family crisis. Picture a parent's reaction to a mediocre report card as akin to discovering you've joined a cult—dramatic, to say the least. The fear of bringing dishonor to one's family can drive people to extreme measures, reinforcing a cycle of shame and anxiety.

I remember when I was in 7th grade, I received a C+ in honors math. For many, a C+ might be a disappointment, but manageable. However, in my household, it was tantamount to a catastrophe. Despite the fact that it was an honors class, which meant the C+ reflected as a B+ in my grade point average, my father and stepmother didn't care. To them, it was a failure. The result? I was grounded to my room in the basement for an entire semester.

Imagine being a seventh grader, full of energy and curiosity, suddenly confined to a cold, dimly lit basement. I wasn't allowed to socialize, go anywhere, or participate in any activities. My life shrank to the four walls of that basement room. The isolation was suffocating, and the message was clear: I had failed them, and therefore, I was undeserving of any joy or freedom.

Being isolated in the basement felt like being exiled. It wasn't just a punishment; it was a statement about my worth. Every day, as I sat alone, I felt the weight of their disappointment pressing down on me. It was as if their disapproval had a physical presence, a constant reminder that I was not good enough. The basement became a symbol of my perceived inadequacy, a place where shame seeped into my bones.

My peers were out living their lives—laughing, playing, experiencing the world—while I was stuck in a cycle of self-doubt and self-criticism. I began to internalize the idea that my value was tied to my academic performance. The pressure to excel was no longer just external; it had become a part of me. I felt like I had to constantly prove my worth, not just to my parents, but to myself.

The emotional impact of that period in the basement lingered long after I was allowed to rejoin the world. The fear of failure, the anxiety of not meeting expectations, and the deep-seated belief that mistakes were unforgivable had taken root. It wasn't just about a single grade; it was about the constant, gnawing fear that I was inherently flawed.

This experience is a stark example of how the pressure to achieve can morph into a source of deep shame. It's not just about the immediate consequences of punishment; it's about the long-lasting impact on self-worth and identity. When achievements are prioritized above all else, the failure to meet those high standards becomes a reflection of personal inadequacy.

In cultures where academic success is so heavily emphasized, the fear of disappointing one's family can lead to extreme actions and profound emotional scars. My time in the basement was not just a punishment for a poor grade—it was a formative experience that shaped my understanding of worth and achievement. It took years to unlearn the lesson that my value was tied to my performance, to recognize that I was more than my grades, and to rebuild my sense of self-worth outside the confines of academic success.

Understanding these cultural and familial pressures is crucial in recognizing the roots of shame and beginning the process of healing. By acknowledging and addressing these patterns, we can start to break the cycle and create a more compassionate, supportive environment for ourselves and future generations.

On the other hand, Western cultures often emphasize individual success and autonomy. This might sound liberating, but it also brings its own brand of pressure. The American Dream, with its promise that anyone can achieve greatness through hard work, can become a source of profound shame if personal achievements don't match societal benchmarks. It's like being told you have a golden ticket to Willy Wonka's factory, but when you get there, the gates are locked because you didn't hustle hard enough.

In the United States, for example, the pressure to succeed financially can overshadow other aspects of life. Success is often measured by the size of your paycheck, the prestige of your job, or the luxury of your possessions. Failure to meet these standards can lead to feelings of inadequacy and shame, as if your worth is tied directly to your bank balance. The cultural narrative implies that if you're not living in a big house with a white picket fence, you're somehow failing at life. This can lead to a relentless pursuit of success, where the fear of falling short becomes a constant companion.

Consider also the cultural quilt squares of Latin American families, where familial bonds and community are central. The expectation to uphold family honor can be just as strong, but it's often intertwined with a deep sense of loyalty and collective responsibility. Failing to contribute to the family's well-being or straying from traditional roles can result in shame and ostracization. It's as if every decision you make is weighed against a scale of cultural and familial expectations, with any deviation viewed as a betrayal.

In the Latino community, family is everything. The concept of "familismo" places a high value on close family relationships, mutual support, and loyalty. This cultural value fosters a strong network of support, but it also brings with it immense pressure to conform to familial and societal expectations. Deviating from these expectations is not just a personal failure; it's seen as a failure to honor and respect the family. This cultural dynamic creates an environment where individuals may sacrifice their personal desires and well-being to meet the collective standards set by their family and community.

My own experience with this cultural dynamic has been deeply personal and eye-opening, particularly through my relationship with my Puerto Rican husband, Vidal. Growing up in a household where family honor and community standing were paramount, he was raised with an acute awareness of his role within the family structure. However, his upbringing was far from the supportive and nurturing environment that such cultural values might suggest.

My husband's father was a bipolar, schizophrenic veteran who regularly cheated on and physically abused his wife, often in front of the children. The trauma of witnessing such violence and instability was compounded by his father's blatant favoritism towards his older brother and younger sister. They were constantly praised, while he was never good enough in his father's eyes. This harsh treatment was partially rooted in the fact that he was born very sick and had numerous operations and treatments for his lungs. His father saw him as invaluable because he couldn't play sports or join the army like his siblings.

Imagine being a child who is already struggling with serious health issues, only to be further burdened by a father's relentless disdain. His father would often remind him that he was a disappointment, that he would never measure up to his siblings. This constant barrage of negativity seeped into my husband's self-perception, reinforcing the idea that he was inherently flawed and unworthy of love and respect. It's like being handed a script in which you are perpetually cast as the failure, with no chance of redemption.

The emotional scars of this upbringing ran deep. While his siblings were groomed to uphold the family's honor through their achievements in sports and the military, he was left to navigate the harsh reality of being deemed "less than." His father's attempts to unalive himself in front of the family added another layer of trauma, embedding the message that life was precarious and fraught with emotional landmines.

Living with my husband, I have seen firsthand how these cultural and familial expectations have shaped his identity and choices. There were times when the weight of his father's words would surface, casting a shadow over his self-esteem and sense of worth. Despite his strengths and accomplishments, the echoes of his father's disdain were never far away. It was as if a part of him was always waiting for the other shoe to drop, for someone to reaffirm that he was not good enough.

Navigating these cultural expectations while building our own lives together has been a delicate balance. Despite the challenges, there is also a profound sense of resilience and support within these cultural frameworks. The same familial bonds that can feel restrictive also provide a network of unwavering support and love. Vidal's family, with all their expectations and pressures, also exemplifies the strength and solidarity that comes from being part of a tightly-knit community. This duality—where love and pressure coexist—defines much of our shared experience.

Reflecting on my own journey and my husband's upbringing, it's clear how deeply cultural values can shape our perceptions of shame and success. Understanding these influences is crucial in recognizing the roots of shame and beginning the process of healing. By acknowledging and addressing these patterns, we can start to break the cycle and create a more compassionate, supportive environment for ourselves.

In Middle Eastern cultures, similar dynamics play out with an emphasis on family honor and societal standing. The concept of 'haram' (forbidden) and 'halal' (permissible) extends beyond religious practices into everyday behavior, creating a framework where actions are constantly judged against moral and social codes. Deviating from these codes can result in intense shame not just for the individual but for the entire family. It's like navigating a minefield where any wrong step can bring disgrace and dishonor.

Even within a single country, subcultures can vary dramatically. In African American communities, for example, historical traumas and systemic oppression have created a unique cultural fabric where resilience and perseverance are celebrated, but there can also be an underlying pressure to rise above the socio-economic challenges. The legacy of struggle and the fight for equality add layers of complexity to the individual and collective experiences of shame and pride.

These cultural threads weave together to create a complex tapestry of expectations and pressures. Understanding the specific patterns and colors of your family's cultural quilt can help you see how shame has been interwoven into your life. It allows you to acknowledge that while some of these pressures are external, others are deeply embedded in the cultural narrative you've inherited.

The first step in this journey is awareness. Take the time to reflect on your family history and the messages you've received about success, failure, and worth. Consider the stories that were told, the behaviors that were modeled, and the values that were emphasized. Were there certain achievements that were celebrated more than others? Were there failures that were met with harsh criticism or silent disapproval? By mapping out these experiences, you can start to see the threads of shame that have been passed down through generations.

Once you've identified these threads, the next step is to examine them closely. This means looking at the origins of these beliefs and behaviors and understanding how they have influenced your life. For example, if you were constantly told that academic success was the only path to worthiness, you might have internalized a fear of failure that affects your decisions and actions even today. By recognizing this, you can start to challenge and change these beliefs.

This process isn't about rejecting your culture or family but about understanding and transforming the harmful patterns that have been passed down. It's like restoring an old quilt—not throwing it away, but carefully repairing the damaged sections so it can continue to provide warmth and comfort without the hidden barbs. This means acknowledging the positive aspects of your cultural heritage while addressing the negative ones. It's about finding a balance between honoring your past and creating a healthier future.

So, as you consider your own family's square in this vast cultural quilt, think about the patterns that have shaped you. Reflect on the historical events, societal norms, and collective values that have influenced your experiences of shame and worthiness. By doing so, you can start to unravel the threads that bind you and reweave your own narrative with intention and compassion.

This is not an easy process, and it can bring up a lot of emotions. You might feel sadness for the pain that your ancestors experienced, anger at the injustices they faced, or relief at finally understanding why you feel the way you do. Allow yourself to feel these emotions without judgment. They are a natural part of the healing process.

As you work through these feelings, it can be helpful to talk to others who understand what you're going through. This might be a therapist, a support group, or trusted friends and family members. Sharing your experiences and hearing others' stories can provide validation and support. It reminds you that you're not alone in this journey.

Another important aspect of this process is self-compassion. Be kind to yourself as you unravel these threads of shame. Recognize that you are doing the best you can with the knowledge and resources you have. Celebrate your progress, no matter how small, and give yourself credit for the courage it takes to face these difficult issues.

By engaging in this work, you are not only healing yourself but also breaking the cycle of shame for future generations. You are creating a new legacy, one that is based on understanding, compassion, and resilience. This is a powerful gift, both to yourself and to those who come after you.

Imagine a future where your children and grandchildren look at their own cultural quilt and see a rich tapestry of strength, love, and support. By addressing the threads of shame now, you are helping to ensure that their experiences will be different. They will inherit a legacy of pride and self-worth, free from the burdens that you have carried.

As you continue this journey, remember that it's not about perfection. There will be setbacks and challenges along the way. But each step you take is a step towards healing and transformation. Keep moving forward with hope and determination, knowing that you are creating a better future for yourself and your family.

So, take a deep breath and look at your family's quilt. See it for what it is—a complex, beautiful, and sometimes painful tapestry of experiences. Embrace the process of understanding and healing, and know that you have the power to change the narrative. You have the strength to transform the threads of shame into a legacy of compassion and resilience. And that, my friend, is something truly worth celebrating.

Practical Exercise: *Family Genogram*

One useful exercise is to create a genogram, a type of family tree that includes emotional relationships and patterns across generations. By mapping out the dynamics and significant events in your family's history, you can gain insight into how shame has been transmitted and start to unravel the threads that bind you.

> **Create Your Genogram:** Draw a family tree that includes at least three generations. Note down key behaviors, attitudes, and messages related to shame and criticism. Include major life events that might have impacted these dynamics.
>
> **Identify Patterns:** Look at your genogram and identify recurring themes and behaviors. How did your grandparents' attitudes affect your parents? How have your parents' behaviors influenced you?
>
> **Journal Your Reflections:** Write about the patterns you've discovered. How have these patterns shaped your identity and self-worth? What steps can you take to break the cycle?
>
> **Share and Discuss:** If possible, share your findings with a trusted friend, family member, or therapist. Discussing these patterns can provide new perspectives and support.

Understanding the intergenerational aspect of shame is a vital step in the healing process. By recognizing the roots of your shame and the cultural factors that reinforce it, you can begin to dismantle the legacy you've inherited. This journey is about reclaiming your narrative, transforming your family's square of the cultural quilt, and creating a new pattern that reflects self-awareness and compassion.

Ready to confront the shadows of your family history and step into the light?

Let's keep moving forward.

CHAPTER 4
AN INTRODUCTION TO THE SHADOW OF SHAME

Shame is a sneaky beast. It has a way of creeping into our thoughts and behaviors, influencing our decisions without us even realizing it. It's like a virus that embeds itself into our psyche, shaping how we see ourselves and interact with the world. The first step in dismantling the power of toxic shame is to recognize its patterns. In this chapter, we're going to help you identify shame-based thoughts and behaviors, and explore how shame manifests in adult relationships and decision-making.

Identifying Shame-Based Thoughts & Behaviors

Let's start with the basics: *what does a shame-based thought look like?* Shame-based thoughts are often irrational and self-critical. They can pop up in various situations, often triggered by something seemingly minor.

Here are some common examples:

Perfectionism: "If I don't do this perfectly, I'm a failure."

People-pleasing: "I have to make everyone happy, or they'll reject me."

Negative self-talk: "I'm so stupid. I can't do anything right."

Catastrophizing: "If I make one mistake, everything will fall apart."

Overgeneralization: "I messed up this project, so I'm a complete disaster in everything."

These thoughts are like mental landmines, ready to explode and reinforce the idea that you are fundamentally flawed. Picture walking through a minefield every day of your life, never knowing when you might step on one. They create a constant state of anxiety and self-doubt, making it difficult to trust yourself and your abilities.

Imagine you're at work, about to present a project you've poured your heart into. As you stand up, ready to shine, a voice in your head whispers, "What if they hate it? What if you mess up?" Suddenly, your confidence wavers. You stumble over your words, not because you don't know your stuff, but because the fear of being judged and found wanting has taken hold. The landmine explodes, and you're left picking up the pieces of your shattered self-esteem.

Or perhaps you're about to ask someone out, someone you've had a crush on for ages. Just as you're about to make your move, the gremlin chimes in, "Why would they ever go out with you? You're not attractive enough, not interesting enough." The anxiety builds, your palms sweat, and instead of striking up a conversation, you retreat, convinced that rejection is inevitable. Another landmine, another hit to your confidence. These mental landmines aren't just isolated incidents; they can form a pervasive pattern that shapes your entire outlook on life. When shame-based thoughts dominate your thinking, they become self-fulfilling prophecies. You start to avoid opportunities, shy away from challenges, and settle for less than you deserve because the fear of failure and rejection is too overwhelming.

This constant state of vigilance takes a toll on your mental health. The anxiety can become so ingrained that you start to believe it's a natural part of who you are. You might develop coping mechanisms to deal with this chronic stress, but often, these are just Band-Aids on a deeper wound. Procrastination, perfectionism, and self-sabotage become your go-to strategies for avoiding the pain of potential failure or rejection.

The worst part? These shame-based thoughts can become so normalized that you stop questioning them.

They blend into the background of your daily life, subtly influencing your decisions and interactions. You might not even realize how much they're holding you back until you take a step back and examine the patterns.

For instance, let's say you're offered a promotion at work. On the surface, you should be thrilled. But instead of celebrating, you find yourself thinking, "What if I can't handle the responsibility? What if I'm not actually good enough for this role?" The excitement is quickly overshadowed by dread, and you might even consider turning down the opportunity because the risk of failing feels too great.

In relationships, these landmines can cause you to misinterpret your partner's actions or words, always fearing the worst. A simple disagreement might spiral into a full-blown argument in your mind, as you start to believe that it's not just about the issue at hand, but about your worthiness as a partner. The fear of being abandoned or rejected can make you clingy or distant, neither of which is conducive to a healthy relationship.

The key to defusing these landmines is awareness and action. By identifying these shame-based thoughts and understanding their origins, you can start to challenge them. It's about reprogramming your mind to recognize that these thoughts are not truths, but distortions. With practice, you can learn to replace these negative patterns with more balanced, self-compassionate thinking.

Now, let's talk about behaviors. Shame-based behaviors are actions that stem from these toxic thoughts.

They are often self-sabotaging and can include:

Avoidance: Staying away from situations where you might fail or be judged. Imagine being invited to a networking event that could potentially advance your career. Instead of seeing it as an opportunity, you focus on the possibility of awkward conversations or saying something foolish. The fear of judgment paralyzes you, and you decide not to go. In doing so, you miss out on valuable connections and opportunities for growth. This avoidance keeps you stuck in your comfort zone, where you feel safe but stagnant.

Procrastination: Putting off tasks because you're afraid you won't do them perfectly. Picture sitting down to write a report for work or school. As you open your laptop, a wave of anxiety washes over you. "What if it's not good enough?" you wonder. The thought of producing anything less than perfect overwhelms you, so you decide to put it off until later. Later turns into hours, then days, and suddenly you're scrambling to finish it at the last minute, reinforcing the belief that you can't handle tasks efficiently.

Self-isolation: Withdrawing from others to avoid the risk of rejection. You might have friends inviting you out for a weekend trip, but instead of feeling excited, you're filled with dread. "What if they don't really want me there? What if I'm just a burden?" you think. To protect yourself from the perceived risk of rejection, you decline the invitation. While this shields you from potential hurt, it also prevents you from forming deeper, meaningful connections, leaving you feeling lonely and disconnected.

Overcompensation: Trying to prove your worth by going above and beyond, often to your own detriment. This might look like taking on extra projects at work, volunteering for every committee, or constantly trying to be the best friend or partner. You're driven by the need to prove that you are valuable, but in doing so, you often neglect your own needs and well-being. It's like running on a treadmill set to an impossible speed—you're exhausting yourself but never feeling like you've done enough.

Approval-seeking: Constantly seeking validation from others to feel worthy. Whether it's fishing for compliments on social media, always asking for feedback, or needing constant reassurance from your partner, this behavior is rooted in the belief that your worth depends on others' opinions. It's a never-ending quest for validation, where each compliment or affirmation is only a temporary fix, never truly filling the void of self-doubt.

Recognizing these thoughts and behaviors is the first step in breaking free from the cycle of shame. It's like turning on the lights in a dark room—once you see the patterns, you can start to change them. Awareness allows you to identify when you're falling into these traps and gives you the power to choose a different path.

Take avoidance, for example. Next time you're faced with a situation that triggers your fear of judgment, acknowledge the fear but challenge it. Remind yourself of past successes and the strengths that you bring to the table. Push yourself to attend that event, engage in that conversation, or take that risk. The more you face these fears head-on, the less power they hold over you.

With procrastination, break tasks into smaller, more manageable steps. Set realistic goals and deadlines for each step, and celebrate small victories along the way. This approach reduces the overwhelming pressure of perfection and helps you build momentum, showing yourself that you can handle tasks effectively.

For self-isolation, start small by accepting invitations or initiating plans with close friends. Gradually expand your social circle, and practice being vulnerable in safe, supportive environments. Remember, true connection comes from being authentic, not perfect.

Overcompensation requires setting boundaries and learning to say no. Recognize that your worth isn't determined by how much you do for others but by who you are. Take time for self-care and prioritize your own needs, understanding that it's okay to take a step back and recharge.

Approval-seeking can be countered by building self-validation practices. Keep a journal where you acknowledge your achievements and positive qualities. Practice self-affirmations and remind yourself that your worth isn't contingent on external validation. Over time, you'll find that you rely less on others' opinions and more on your own sense of self-worth.

Changing these patterns isn't easy, and it doesn't happen overnight. But with awareness, intention, and practice, you can start to break free from the cycle of shame and create healthier, more fulfilling behaviors. It's about reclaiming your power and recognizing that you are enough, just as you are.

How Shame Manifests in Adult Relationships

Shame doesn't just affect how we see ourselves; it also has a profound impact on our relationships. When you carry toxic shame, it's like bringing an invisible weight into every interaction.

Here's how it often plays out:

> **Fear of Intimacy:** Shame makes it difficult to get close to others because you fear they'll see the "real" you and reject you. You might keep people at arm's length, avoid deep conversations, or struggle to be vulnerable. Imagine starting to date someone new. At first, everything is exciting and light, but as things start to get serious, you find yourself pulling back. You avoid discussing your feelings or sharing personal stories because the fear of being seen and subsequently rejected is too great. Instead of deepening the relationship, you keep things superficial, ensuring that no one gets close enough to see the parts of you that you believe are unworthy.

People-Pleasing: In relationships, this manifests as always putting others' needs before your own, avoiding conflict at all costs, and constantly seeking approval. It's a way of ensuring that others don't abandon you, but it comes at the cost of your own needs and well-being. Picture yourself in a friendship where you're always the one who compromises. If your friend wants to go to a restaurant you dislike, you agree without hesitation. If there's a conflict, you immediately apologize, even if you're not at fault. Over time, you start to feel resentful and exhausted, but the fear of losing the relationship keeps you stuck in this pattern. Your needs and desires become secondary, leading to an imbalance that strains the relationship.

Control Issues: To avoid feeling vulnerable, you might try to control every aspect of your relationships. This can include being overly critical, micromanaging, or trying to dictate how others should behave. For example, in a romantic relationship, you might insist on knowing your partner's whereabouts at all times, or you might criticize the way they do simple tasks, like cooking or cleaning. This need for control is a defense mechanism to prevent any surprises that might make you feel vulnerable. While it might give you a temporary sense of security, it erodes trust and intimacy, pushing your partner away and creating a cycle of tension and dissatisfaction.

Jealousy and Insecurity: Shame makes you doubt your worth, leading to feelings of jealousy and insecurity in your relationships. You might constantly compare yourself to others, feel threatened by your partner's interactions with others, or need constant reassurance. Imagine being in a relationship where every time your partner talks to someone attractive, you feel a pang of jealousy. You start to question your own attractiveness and worth, leading to accusations and mistrust. This insecurity can become suffocating for both you and your partner, as you require constant reassurance and validation, which strains the relationship and erodes its foundation.

Withdrawing or Shutting Down: When faced with conflict or criticism, you might withdraw or shut down emotionally to protect yourself from further shame. This can create distance and communication barriers in your relationships. Think about a time when you had an argument with a loved one. Instead of discussing the issue, you retreat into silence, building walls around your emotions. You might avoid the person for days, hoping the problem will disappear on its own. This withdrawal doesn't resolve the conflict; it only creates more distance and misunderstanding. Over time, this pattern of shutting down can lead to a lack of emotional intimacy and connection, making it difficult to sustain a healthy relationship.

Recognizing these patterns in your relationships is crucial for breaking the cycle of shame.

Here are some steps to help you start changing these behaviors:

1. **Self-Awareness:** Pay attention to your thoughts and behaviors in relationships. Notice when you're avoiding intimacy, people-pleasing, trying to control, feeling jealous, or withdrawing. Journaling can be a helpful tool for tracking these patterns.

2. **Communication:** Practice open and honest communication with your partner, friends, or family. Share your fears and insecurities, and let them know how they can support you. This vulnerability can strengthen your relationships and build trust.

3. **Setting Boundaries:** Learn to set healthy boundaries that protect your well-being. This means saying no when you need to, expressing your needs, and not compromising your values to please others.

4. **Building Self-Compassion:** Develop a kinder relationship with yourself. Challenge the negative self-talk and replace it with affirmations that reinforce your worth and value. Remember, you are deserving of love and respect, just as you are.

5. **Therapy:** Consider seeking professional help to work through deep-seated shame and its impact on

your relationships. A therapist can provide valuable insights and strategies for healing and growth.

By recognizing and addressing these shame-based behaviors, you can begin to cultivate healthier, more fulfilling relationships. It's a journey of self-discovery and empowerment, where you learn to embrace your true self and build connections based on authenticity and mutual respect.

Shame in Decision-Making

Shame doesn't just stop at relationships; it also influences our decision-making processes.

Here's how:

Risk Aversion: Shame makes you fear failure, so you avoid taking risks. This can limit your opportunities and keep you stuck in a comfort zone that's anything but comfortable. Imagine you have a brilliant idea for a new business venture. Deep down, you know it has potential, but the fear of failing and being judged holds you back. You convince yourself that it's safer to stick with your current job, even though it doesn't fulfill you. This avoidance of risk might keep you safe from immediate failure, but it also keeps you from realizing your full potential and achieving your dreams. You end up stuck in a monotonous routine, constantly wondering "what if."

Overthinking and Paralysis: You might overanalyze every decision, worried about making the "wrong" choice. This can lead to decision paralysis, where you're so afraid of making a mistake that you end up doing nothing. Picture being offered two job opportunities. Instead of feeling excited, you're paralyzed by the fear of choosing the wrong one. You list endless pros and cons, seek advice from everyone you know, and still can't make a decision. The deadlines pass, and both opportunities slip away, leaving you stuck in the same place, regretting your inaction. This paralysis stems from the shame-based belief that making a wrong choice would confirm your inadequacy.

Self-Sabotage: Sometimes, shame convinces you that you don't deserve success or happiness, leading you to make choices that undermine your own goals and desires. This can include procrastinating, missing deadlines, or quitting projects prematurely. You might finally start that book you've always wanted to write, but halfway through, the voice of shame whispers, "Who do you think you are? You're not a real writer." You procrastinate, miss deadlines, and eventually abandon the project. Self-sabotage is a way of protecting yourself from the potential pain of failure or rejection by preemptively proving to yourself that you were right all along about your lack of worth.

People-Pleasing Decisions: You might make choices based on what others want or expect from you, rather than what's best for you. This can lead to resentment and unfulfilled potential. Suppose your family wants you to pursue a career in medicine, but your passion lies in the arts. Driven by the desire to please them and avoid conflict, you enroll in medical school. Years later, you find yourself deeply unhappy, feeling trapped in a career that was never your own choice. The resentment builds, not just towards your family, but also towards yourself for not standing up for your own dreams. This people-pleasing behavior is rooted in the fear that being true to yourself will lead to rejection and disapproval.

Recognizing these shame-based decision-making patterns is crucial for breaking free from their grip.

Here are some steps to help you start making decisions that align with your true self:

1. **Self-Reflection:** Take time to reflect on your past decisions. Identify moments where shame influenced your choices. Understanding the why behind your decisions can help you make more conscious choices in the future.

2. **Small Risks:** Start by taking small risks in a controlled manner. This could be trying a new hobby, speaking up in a meeting, or sharing an idea with a friend. These small steps build confidence and show you that failure isn't the end of the world.

3. **Mindfulness:** Practice mindfulness to stay present and reduce overthinking. Techniques such as deep breathing, meditation, and journaling can help you stay grounded and focused on the here and now, rather than getting lost in a spiral of what-ifs.

4. **Challenge Negative Thoughts:** When self-sabotaging thoughts arise, challenge them. Ask yourself if these thoughts are based on facts or on the irrational fears that shame has instilled in you. Reframe them with more balanced, positive affirmations.

5. **Set Boundaries**: Learn to set boundaries with others. Understand that it's okay to prioritize your needs and desires. Making decisions based on what's best for you isn't selfish; it's essential for your well-being.

6. **Seek Support:** Surround yourself with supportive people who encourage you to take risks and follow your passions. Sometimes an outside perspective can help you see the possibilities that shame has obscured.

7. **Visualize Success:** Instead of focusing on potential failure, visualize what success would look like. Picture yourself achieving your goals and the positive impact it would have on your life. This shift in focus can help mitigate the fear of failure.

By recognizing and addressing these shame-based decision-making patterns, you can start making choices that reflect your true desires and values. It's about reclaiming your power and understanding that you are capable and deserving of success and happiness. It's about learning to trust yourself and your instincts, and understanding that mistakes are a natural part of growth, not a reflection of your worth.

Addressing shame patterns is a vital step in the journey toward healing and self-acceptance. By shining a light on these shadows, you can begin to dismantle the distortions that have held you back and reclaim your true self. Remember, this is a process, and it takes time and effort. Be patient with yourself and know that you are worthy of love, acceptance, and happiness.

As we move forward, we'll continue to explore strategies for overcoming shame and building resilience. Together, we'll uncover the strength within you to break free from the chains of toxic shame and embrace a life of authenticity and self-worth.

Practical Exercises

To help you identify and address shame-based thoughts and behaviors, here are a few practical exercises:

Thought Journaling: Keep a journal where you write down negative thoughts as they occur. Next to each thought, write a more balanced and compassionate response. Over time, this can help rewire your thinking patterns.

Mindfulness Meditation: Practice mindfulness to become more aware of your thoughts and feelings without judgment. This can help you recognize when shame is influencing your behavior and make more conscious choices.

Affirmations: Create a list of positive affirmations that counteract your shame-based thoughts. Repeat these affirmations daily to reinforce a healthier self-image.

Role-Playing: Practice role-playing different scenarios with a trusted friend or therapist. This can help you build confidence in setting boundaries, expressing your needs, and challenging shame-based behaviors.

Self-Compassion Exercises: Engage in activities that promote self-compassion, such as writing yourself a letter of kindness, practicing self-care, and celebrating your achievements, no matter how small.

Recognizing and addressing shame patterns is a vital step in the journey toward healing and self-acceptance. By shining a light on these shadows, you can begin to dismantle the distortions that have held you back and reclaim your true self. Remember, this is a process, and it takes time and effort. Be patient with yourself and know that you are worthy of love, acceptance, and happiness.

As we move forward, we'll continue to explore strategies for overcoming shame and building resilience. Together, we'll uncover the strength within you to break free from the chains of toxic shame and embrace a life of authenticity and self-worth.

CHAPTER 5
THE PATH TO HEALING

Welcome to the chapter where we roll up our sleeves and get to the nitty-gritty of healing from toxic shame. If you've stuck with me this far, congratulations. It means you're ready to face the gremlins head-on and reclaim your life. It's not going to be easy, and it's definitely not going to be pretty, but hey, if Frodo can carry that ring to Mordor, you can tackle your shame.

Healing from shame is a journey, not a destination. It requires patience, persistence, and a hefty dose of self-compassion. Think of it as a long road trip—there will be detours, pit stops, and maybe a few wrong turns, but with a reliable map and some good tunes, you'll get there. This chapter is your roadmap, complete with strategies, tools, and a playlist of self-compassion anthems to keep you company along the way.

First, let's acknowledge the courage it takes to even consider facing your shame. It's like deciding to clean out a cluttered attic—daunting, dusty, and full of things you'd rather not deal with. But once you start, you'll find forgotten treasures among the junk, and the weight of all that clutter will begin to lift. So, let's open the door, turn on the lights, and start sorting through the mess.

Let's talk about some concrete strategies to overcome shame. These are the tools you'll need to start dismantling the shame fortress brick by brick. Think of this as your personal toolkit for battling those shame gremlins that have been living rent-free in your head for far too long. Each strategy is designed to help you take back control, challenge negative thoughts, and build a more compassionate relationship with yourself.

Imagine you're embarking on a home renovation project. Your inner world is the house, and shame has turned it into a fixer-upper nightmare. There are broken windows of self-doubt, leaky roofs of insecurity, and a foundation cracked by years of toxic beliefs. But with the right tools, you can transform this dilapidated structure into a cozy, self-loving sanctuary.

The first step in overcoming shame is to recognize when it's happening. Pay attention to the thoughts and feelings that arise when you're in shame's grip. Are you feeling unworthy, flawed, or not good enough? Once you identify these feelings, give them a name. Naming your shame can help you gain perspective and separate it from your identity. It's like calling out Voldemort by his name instead of referring to him as "He-Who-Must-Not-Be-Named." It takes away some of its power.

Recognizing shame means becoming aware of those moments when your inner critic goes on a rampage. It's that nagging voice telling you that you're not smart enough, attractive enough, or successful enough. Instead of letting these thoughts run amok, pause and identify them for what they are: manifestations of shame. By naming them, you're taking the first step toward disarming them.

Once you've identified shame, it's time to challenge those thoughts. Ask yourself, "Is this really true?" Often, shame-based thoughts are distortions of reality. For example, if you think, "I'm a failure because I didn't get that promotion," challenge it by listing your achievements and strengths. Remember, Harry Potter didn't become a hero because he never failed; he became a hero because he kept going despite his failures.

Challenging shame-based thoughts involves playing detective with your own mind. Look for evidence that contradicts these negative beliefs. If you're thinking, "I'm terrible at my job," recall moments when you received praise or accomplished a difficult task. By actively disputing these thoughts, you can start to rewrite the narrative in your head from one of shame to one of resilience and competence.

Shame thrives in secrecy. Find a trusted friend, therapist, or support group where you can share your experiences. Speaking your shame out loud can diminish its power and help you realize you're not alone. It's like that scene in every horror movie where the protagonist finally turns on the lights and sees that the monster isn't as terrifying as they thought.

Opening up about your shame can feel like standing naked in front of an audience—it's vulnerable and terrifying.

But sharing your experiences with someone you trust can be incredibly liberating. When you speak your shame, you bring it out of the shadows and into the light. You'll often find that others have experienced similar feelings, which can help you feel less isolated and more understood.

Treat yourself with the same kindness and understanding you would offer a friend. When you make a mistake, instead of beating yourself up, remind yourself that everyone makes mistakes. You're not a robot programmed for perfection; you're a wonderfully flawed human being, just like the rest of us.

Self-compassion is like giving your inner child a warm hug. It means acknowledging your pain and offering yourself comfort instead of criticism. When you slip up, instead of saying, "I'm such an idiot," try saying, "I'm having a tough time, and that's okay." This shift in perspective can help you move from self-judgment to self-kindness, which is crucial for healing shame.

Cultivate a supportive inner dialogue by regularly practicing positive affirmations and self-talk. Replace negative, shame-based thoughts with affirming statements about your worth and capabilities. For example, instead of thinking, "I'll never be good enough," try, "I am worthy and capable just as I am." It's like reprogramming your mental software to run on love and acceptance instead of shame and self-criticism.

Start each day by affirming your worth and capabilities. Write down affirmations and place them where you'll see them often—on your bathroom mirror, your fridge, or your computer screen. Over time, these positive messages can help shift your mindset from one dominated by shame to one anchored in self-worth.

Sometimes, overcoming shame requires professional guidance. Therapists and counselors can provide valuable tools and insights tailored to your specific needs. They can help you navigate the complex emotions and patterns that contribute to your shame. Think of therapy as hiring an expert contractor to help with your renovation project—they have the skills and experience to address issues you might struggle to tackle on your own.

Professional help isn't a sign of weakness; it's a powerful step toward healing. Therapists can offer a safe space to explore your feelings and develop strategies for managing shame. They can also help you uncover and address the root causes of your shame, leading to deeper, more lasting healing.

Accept that imperfection is a natural part of the human experience. Striving for perfection is not only unrealistic but also a significant contributor to shame. Embrace your flaws and mistakes as opportunities for growth and learning. Remember, even the most beautiful quilts have irregular stitches and unique patterns—these imperfections make them unique and valuable.

Embracing imperfection means letting go of the need to be flawless. It's about recognizing that your worth isn't tied to your achievements or the absence of mistakes. Instead, it's rooted in your inherent humanity and the unique qualities that make you who you are. Gratitude can be a powerful antidote to shame. Regularly reflecting on the things you're thankful for can help shift your focus from what's wrong in your life to what's right. Keep a gratitude journal where you jot down three things you're grateful for each day. Over time, this practice can help rewire your brain to notice and appreciate the positive aspects of your life, reducing the hold of shame.

Gratitude isn't about ignoring your struggles; it's about balancing them with an awareness of the good things in your life. By practicing gratitude, you can create a more balanced, positive perspective that counteracts the negative effects of shame.

Building Self-Compassion

Self-compassion is like the Patronus charm for shame—it protects and empowers you. When you practice self-compassion, you develop a shield against the negative, shame-based thoughts that try to bring you down.

Here's how to build it:

Mindfulness
Be present with your emotions without judgment. Notice your feelings and acknowledge them without letting them define you. It's like watching a storm pass by; you observe the rain and wind, knowing it will eventually clear. Mindfulness is all about staying present and aware of what's happening in the moment. When you feel shame creeping in, take a deep breath and pause. Notice the physical sensations in your body—is your heart racing? Are your palms sweaty? Pay attention to these signs without judgment. It's like being a neutral observer of your own experience.

Try this: the next time you're overwhelmed by shame, find a quiet space and close your eyes. Take a few deep breaths and bring your focus to the present moment. Acknowledge your feelings—"I'm feeling ashamed right now"—without trying to change them. Imagine your emotions as clouds passing through the sky, coming and going without staying forever. This practice can help you detach from the intensity of your emotions and see them as temporary states, not defining truths.

Common Humanity
Remind yourself that everyone struggles. You're not alone in your experiences. This shared understanding can help you feel connected rather than isolated. Think about it: even Beyoncé probably has days where she feels less than flawless. Common humanity is recognizing that suffering and imperfection are part of the human experience. When you're caught in a shame spiral, it's easy to feel like you're the only one who's ever messed up. But the truth is, everyone has their own battles. Remembering this can help you feel less isolated and more connected to others.

Try this: when you make a mistake or feel ashamed, think about someone you admire. Imagine them dealing with a similar issue. Realize that they, too, have moments of doubt and imperfection. Visualize them navigating these struggles with grace and resilience. This exercise can remind you that you're not alone and that struggling doesn't make you any less worthy.

Self-Kindness
Speak to yourself kindly, especially during tough times. Instead of saying, "I'm such an idiot," try, "I made a mistake, and that's okay." It's the difference between giving yourself a hug and kicking yourself when you're down. Choose the hug. Self-kindness means treating yourself with the same care and compassion that you would offer a dear friend. When you catch yourself in negative self-talk, pause and reframe your thoughts. Instead of being your harshest critic, become your own biggest supporter.

Try this: create a list of kind phrases you can use when you're feeling down.

Here are a few to get you started:

> **"I'm doing the best I can, and that's enough."**
>
> **"It's okay to make mistakes; they're part of learning."**
>
> **"I deserve love and compassion, especially from myself."**

Keep this list handy and refer to it whenever you're tempted to be hard on yourself. Over time, these kinder thoughts can become your default response to difficult situations.

Building self-compassion is a journey, much like learning a new skill. It takes practice and patience, but the rewards are profound. When you cultivate self-compassion, you create a supportive inner environment that nurtures growth and resilience. It's like planting a garden in your soul, where love and acceptance can flourish and outshine the weeds of shame.

Remember, self-compassion is not about letting yourself off the hook or avoiding responsibility. It's about acknowledging your imperfections and treating yourself with the kindness and understanding you deserve. It's about being a good friend to yourself, especially when times are tough.

As you cultivate self-compassion, you'll find it easier to navigate life's challenges with resilience and grace. But self-compassion alone isn't enough; you also need practical tools to manage stress and emotional pain. This is where healthy coping mechanisms come in. By integrating these strategies into your daily routine, you can build a robust toolkit to support your mental and emotional well-being.

Introducing Healthy Coping Mechanisms

Coping mechanisms are like the Swiss Army knife of emotional resilience—they help you navigate life's challenges with more ease.

Here are some healthy ones to add to your toolkit:

Journaling
Writing down your thoughts and feelings can help you process and understand them better. It's like having a conversation with yourself without the risk of being interrupted by your annoying inner critic. When you journal, you give yourself a safe space to explore your emotions, track your progress, and gain insights into your patterns and triggers.

Try this: Set aside 10-15 minutes each day to write in your journal. You don't need a fancy notebook—any blank page will do. Write about whatever comes to mind, whether it's the events of the day, your current feelings, or reflections on past experiences. Don't worry about grammar or spelling; just let your thoughts flow. Over time, you'll find that journaling helps you make sense of your emotions and can provide clarity during tough times.

Physical Activity
Exercise can boost your mood and reduce stress. Whether it's yoga, running, or dancing like no one's watching, find an activity that makes you feel good and stick with it. Remember Elle Woods from "Legally Blonde"? Exercise gives you endorphins, and endorphins make you happy. Plus, regular physical activity can improve your overall health and well-being.

Try this: Experiment with different types of exercise until you find something you enjoy. If you're not a fan of the gym, try going for a hike, taking a dance class, or following a yoga video at home. The key is to find something that feels fun and invigorating, rather than a chore. Aim for at least 30 minutes of activity most days of the week to reap the mental and physical benefits.

Creative Expression
Engage in activities that allow you to express yourself creatively, whether it's painting, writing, or playing music. Creativity can be a powerful outlet for processing emotions and building self-esteem. Think of it as your own version of the "Art Attack" show, minus the giant glue stick. Creative expression allows you to channel your feelings into something tangible and beautiful.

Try this: Set aside time each week for a creative activity that you love. Don't worry about being "good" at it—focus on the joy of creating. Whether it's doodling in a sketchbook, writing poetry, or strumming a guitar, let yourself get lost in the process. You might even want to try something new, like pottery or photography, to keep things fresh and exciting.

Mindfulness and Meditation
These practices can help you stay grounded and present. Apps like Headspace or Calm offer guided meditations that can help you develop a regular practice. It's like hitting the reset button on your brain, giving you a fresh start. Mindfulness and

meditation can reduce stress, increase self-awareness, and improve emotional regulation.

Try this: Start with just a few minutes of meditation each day. Find a quiet space, sit comfortably, and focus on your breath. If your mind wanders, gently bring your attention back to your breathing. Over time, gradually increase the length of your meditation sessions. You can also incorporate mindfulness into daily activities, like eating or walking, by paying full attention to the experience and your sensations.

Connection
Spend time with people who uplift and support you. Social connections can provide a sense of belonging and reduce feelings of shame. Remember the Golden Girls? They had each other's backs, and so should your friends. Building and maintaining supportive relationships is crucial for your mental and emotional well-being.

Try this: Make an effort to connect with friends and family regularly, even if it's just a quick phone call or text. Plan activities that you enjoy together, like movie nights, dinners, or outdoor adventures. If you're looking to expand your social circle, consider joining clubs, volunteering, or taking classes to meet like-minded people. Surround yourself with those who encourage and support you, and be that source of support for others as well.

By integrating these healthy coping mechanisms into your daily routine, you'll build a stronger foundation of emotional resilience and well-being. Remember, it's not about doing everything perfectly—it's about finding what works for you and making small, consistent efforts to take care of yourself.

Healing from toxic shame is a journey, not a sprint. It's about taking small, consistent steps towards building a healthier relationship with yourself. By recognizing and challenging shame, practicing self-compassion, and adopting healthy coping mechanisms, you can start to dismantle the walls shame has built around you.Remember, you're not alone in this journey. We're all a little messy, a little flawed, and a lot deserving of love and compassion. So, keep going, stay kind to yourself, and know that you're doing the best you can. After all, even Frodo needed a Samwise Gamgee to get to Mordor. Surround yourself with your own fellowship and take it one step at a time.

Let's continue this journey.
Onward!

CHAPTER 6
BUILDING RESILIENCE

Resilience is the secret sauce that helps you navigate life's inevitable ups and downs. It's what allows you to keep going when the going gets tough and to rise stronger from the ashes of adversity. When it comes to overcoming shame, resilience is your best ally. It's the armor that shields you from the slings and arrows of toxic thoughts and the fuel that keeps you moving forward.

Shame has a way of knocking you down and making you feel like you'll never get back up. It whispers lies about your worth and capabilities, convincing you that you're fundamentally flawed. But resilience is the antidote to these lies. It's the inner strength that helps you stand back up, dust yourself off, and keep moving forward, no matter how many times you fall.

Think of resilience as your emotional immune system. Just as your physical immune system fights off infections and keeps you healthy, your emotional resilience helps you fend off the negative impacts of shame and other emotional stressors. It allows you to adapt to challenges, recover from setbacks, and maintain a sense of hope and purpose.

Resilience doesn't mean you'll never experience hardship or pain again. It means that when those inevitable challenges arise, you'll have the inner resources to cope, recover, and even grow from the experience. It's about learning to dance in the rain rather than waiting for the storm to pass. Resilience transforms adversity into an opportunity for growth and self-discovery.

Consider resilience like a muscle. The more you exercise it, the stronger it becomes. Each time you face a challenge and choose to persevere, you're strengthening your resilience. This doesn't mean ignoring your pain or pretending everything is okay when it's not. Instead, it's about acknowledging your feelings, processing them, and then finding a way to move forward.

Imagine you're a character in a video game, and resilience is your power-up. Each time you face an obstacle and use resilience, you level up. The challenges don't necessarily get easier, but you get better at handling them. You gain new skills, insights, and strengths that you carry with you into future battles.

Resilience also involves a degree of flexibility. It's not about rigidly sticking to a plan despite all odds; it's about being adaptable and open to change. Life rarely goes exactly as we plan, and resilience allows us to pivot and adjust our course when necessary. It's about finding new paths to our goals when the original ones are blocked.

Think of resilience as your internal GPS. When you encounter a roadblock, it recalculates and helps you find an alternative route. It keeps you moving forward, even if the journey takes longer than expected or requires a few detours. Resilience helps you maintain your sense of direction and purpose, no matter what obstacles arise.

Resilience is also deeply connected to hope. It's the belief that no matter how difficult things are right now, they can and will get better. This hope fuels your determination and gives you the strength to keep going. It's like a lighthouse guiding you through the darkest nights, reminding you that there's light ahead.

Building resilience isn't just about bouncing back from setbacks; it's about bouncing forward. It's about using your experiences of shame and adversity as stepping stones to become a stronger, wiser, and more compassionate version of yourself. It's about transforming pain into power and struggle into strength.

As we move forward in this chapter, we'll explore practical techniques for cultivating resilience. These tools will help you build the inner strength and flexibility needed to overcome shame and thrive despite life's challenges.

Techniques for Cultivating Resilience

Building resilience is like preparing for a long journey. It requires time, effort, and consistent practice. Resilience isn't a trait you're born with; it's a skill you can develop and hone. Think of it as your emotional endurance—each step you take strengthens your ability to face and overcome challenges.

Resilience equips you with the ability to adapt to life's inevitable setbacks, recover from difficulties, and continue moving forward with a sense of purpose and hope. It's about transforming obstacles into opportunities and using adversity as a springboard for growth. By integrating resilience-building techniques into your daily routine, you can enhance your capacity to cope with stress, bounce back from hardships, and maintain a positive outlook.

Ready to embark on this journey of self-discovery and empowerment? *Here are some effective techniques to help you cultivate resilience:*

Develop a Growth Mindset

A growth mindset is the belief that your abilities and intelligence can be developed through effort, learning, and persistence. Embracing a growth mindset helps you view challenges as opportunities for growth rather than as threats to your self-worth.

Try this: When you encounter a difficult situation, ask yourself, "What can I learn from this?" Instead of focusing on the potential for failure, focus on the opportunity to grow and improve. Remember, even superheroes have origin stories filled with challenges and setbacks.

Practice Self-Care

Taking care of your physical, emotional, and mental well-being is crucial for building resilience. Self-care isn't just about bubble baths and spa days (though those are nice too); it's about making choices that nourish and support your overall health.

Try this: Make a list of self-care activities that rejuvenate you. This could include exercise, reading a good book, spending time in nature, or connecting with loved ones. Schedule regular time for these activities and treat them as non-negotiable appointments with yourself.

Set Realistic Goals
Setting and achieving small, realistic goals can boost your confidence and sense of accomplishment. These goals act as stepping stones, helping you build momentum and resilience over time.

Try this: Break down larger goals into smaller, manageable tasks. Celebrate each small victory along the way. Remember, Rome wasn't built in a day, and neither is resilience. Every small step counts.

Build a Support Network
Having a strong support network is essential for resilience. Surround yourself with people who uplift and encourage you. These relationships provide emotional support, practical help, and a sense of belonging.

Try this: Reach out to friends, family, or support groups. Share your experiences and listen to theirs. Mutual support can create a powerful sense of community and resilience. Think of it as your own personal Avengers team—stronger together than apart.

Embrace Flexibility

Resilience involves being adaptable and flexible in the face of change and uncertainty. Instead of rigidly sticking to a plan, be willing to pivot and adjust as needed.

Try this: Practice going with the flow and accepting that not everything will go as planned. When faced with unexpected challenges, take a deep breath and ask yourself, "What's the next best step I can take?" Flexibility can turn obstacles into opportunities.

As you navigate through life's unpredictabilities with resilience, it's also essential to reflect on your past experiences. By doing so, you can uncover valuable lessons and recognize the strength you've built along the way.

Reframing Past Experiences as Sources of Strength

One of the most powerful ways to build resilience is to reframe past experiences of shame and adversity as sources of strength. Instead of viewing these experiences as proof of your inadequacy, see them as evidence of your resilience and growth.

Identify Lessons Learned
Reflect on past challenges and identify the lessons you've learned from them. Every setback is an opportunity for growth and self-discovery.

Try this: Write down a list of past experiences where you felt ashamed or defeated. Next to each one, write down what you learned from that experience. How did it shape you? How did it make you stronger?

Celebrate Your Strengths
Acknowledge the strengths and qualities that helped you overcome past difficulties. Recognizing these strengths can boost your confidence and resilience.

Try this: Make a list of your strengths and accomplishments. Reflect on times when you demonstrated resilience, courage, and perseverance. Keep this list handy as a reminder of your inner strength.

Share Your Story
Sharing your story with others can be a powerful way to reframe your experiences. It allows you to connect with others, find common ground, and inspire resilience in both yourself and others.

Try this: Find a safe space to share your story, whether it's with a trusted friend, a support group, or through writing. Sharing your journey can help you see it from a new perspective and recognize the strength it took to get through it.

Building resilience is an ongoing journey, but it's one that's worth every step. It's not about quick fixes or overnight transformations; it's about the steady, persistent effort to grow stronger and more adaptable over time. By developing a growth mindset, practicing self-care, setting realistic goals, building a support network, embracing flexibility, and reframing past experiences, you can cultivate the resilience needed to overcome shame and thrive in the face of adversity.

Resilience is not about being invincible; it's about finding your inner strength to face life's challenges head-on and emerge even stronger. It's the quiet confidence that whispers, "You can do this," even when the world feels overwhelming. You have the power within you to rise above shame, to transform pain into purpose, and to live a life filled with hope and self-compassion.

So, here's to the brave souls who dare to confront their shame and embrace their resilience. Keep moving forward, one step at a time, knowing that every step you take brings you closer to the life you deserve. Trust in your ability to overcome whatever challenges come your way, and remember that each stumble is an opportunity to rise again, wiser and more determined.

Onward and upward, resilient warrior. Your journey to resilience is not just beginning—it's already underway.

Embrace it with courage and determination, and watch as you transform your life from the inside out.

CHAPTER 7
RECLAIMING IDENTITY

Trauma and shame can leave you feeling like a stranger in your own skin. They distort your sense of self, making you question your worth and identity. But here's the good news: your true self is still there, waiting to be rediscovered and embraced. Reclaiming your identity is a powerful step in the healing journey, allowing you to define who you are outside of the shadows of trauma and family narratives.

Imagine waking up one day and looking in the mirror, only to see a stranger staring back at you. This is what it can feel like when shame and trauma have clouded your sense of self. These experiences can strip away your confidence and leave you feeling disconnected from who you truly are. But deep within you, beneath the layers of pain and doubt, your authentic self remains intact, waiting for you to peel back the layers and reconnect with your true essence.

Reclaiming your identity is not about becoming someone new; it's about rediscovering and embracing the person you've always been. It's about taking back the narrative of your life from the grip of trauma and writing your own story, one that reflects your values, passions, and dreams. This process of self-discovery is a journey—a courageous, sometimes challenging, but ultimately empowering journey that leads to a deeper understanding and acceptance of yourself.

Think of this journey as an archaeological dig. You are the archaeologist, and your mission is to uncover the hidden treasures buried within. These treasures are the pieces of your true self—your values, passions, strengths, and dreams—that have been buried under the rubble of trauma and shame. With each layer you uncover, you get closer to the core of who you are.

This journey requires patience and compassion. It's about exploring different facets of yourself with curiosity and openness, understanding that each piece you uncover is a vital part of your identity. It's about embracing your imperfections and recognizing that they make you unique and beautiful. As you embark on this journey, you'll begin to see that your past experiences, no matter how painful, have shaped you into the resilient and courageous person you are today.

Reclaiming your identity also involves letting go of the narratives imposed on you by others—family, society, and trauma itself. It's about defining yourself on your own terms, free from the expectations and judgments of those who have tried to mold you into someone you're not. It's about standing in your truth and owning your story, unapologetically.

The journey of reclaiming your identity is not a linear path; it's a winding road with twists and turns, highs and lows. There will be moments of clarity and moments of confusion, times of progress and times of setback. But each step you take brings you closer to your authentic self, and each discovery you make strengthens your sense of identity and purpose.

Now, let's explore how you can begin this transformative journey of self-discovery and reclaim your identity post-trauma.

The Process of Self-Discovery Post-Trauma

Self-discovery after trauma is like piecing together a puzzle, only someone threw away the box and the dog chewed up a few pieces. It requires patience, curiosity, and a willingness to explore different facets of yourself. Each piece you uncover brings you closer to understanding who you truly are, beyond the influence of trauma and shame. This process can be both challenging and rewarding, as it involves delving into your past, examining your present, and envisioning your future.

Embarking on this journey of self-discovery means acknowledging the impact of trauma while not allowing it to define you. It's about recognizing that while your experiences have shaped you, they do not determine your worth or your potential. This journey is about reclaiming the narrative of your life and redefining it in a way that aligns with your true self.

Imagine self-discovery as an adventure into the unknown territories of your soul. You're Indiana Jones, but instead of chasing after lost artifacts, you're uncovering hidden treasures within yourself. These treasures are the pieces of your true self—your values, passions, strengths, and dreams—that have been buried under the rubble of trauma and shame. With each layer you uncover, you get closer to the core of who you are.

This journey requires a balance of self-reflection and action. It involves looking inward to understand your thoughts, feelings, and motivations, and then taking concrete steps to align your life with your authentic self. It's about asking yourself the tough questions and being honest with the answers, even when they're uncomfortable. It's about giving yourself permission to grow, change, and evolve.

Think of self-discovery like peeling an onion. There might be some tears, and it can get a little messy, but each layer you peel away reveals more about your true self. Plus, onions add flavor, and so does understanding yourself—spicy, tear-jerking flavor.

As you navigate this path, keep in mind that it's less about a grand destination and more about the journey itself. You're not just finding out who you are; you're becoming who you are meant to be.

So, grab your fedora and whip (or maybe just a journal and some comfy pants), and let's dive into some practical steps to guide you on this transformative journey:

Reflect on Your Values and Beliefs

Start by examining what truly matters to you. Trauma and shame often impose values and beliefs that aren't your own. Take time to reflect on your core values—those fundamental principles that guide your decisions and behavior. What do you believe in? What principles do you want to live by?

Identifying your values is the first step in aligning your life with your true self.

Try this: Write down a list of values that resonate with you. These might include honesty, compassion, creativity, independence, or adventure. Think about moments in your life when you felt most aligned with these values. How can you incorporate them more fully into your daily life?

Explore Your Passions and Interests
Trauma can suppress your interests and passions, making you forget the activities that once brought you joy. Reconnecting with these passions is crucial for rediscovering your identity. What activities make you lose track of time? What subjects ignite your curiosity? Exploring these interests can help you reconnect with your authentic self.

Try this: Create a list of activities or subjects that you've always been curious about or enjoyed. Dedicate time each week to explore one of these interests, whether it's through reading, taking a class, or simply experimenting on your own. Allow yourself to be playful and open-minded in this exploration.

Listen to Your Inner Voice
Your inner voice, or intuition, is a powerful guide to your true self. Trauma and shame can drown out this voice, replacing it with doubt and negativity.

Reclaiming your identity involves tuning back into this inner guidance and trusting your instincts.

Try this: Practice mindfulness or meditation to quiet the noise of external influences and reconnect with your inner voice. When faced with decisions, take a moment to pause and listen to what your intuition is telling you. Trust that this voice is leading you towards your authentic path.

Set Boundaries
Setting boundaries is essential for protecting your reclaimed identity. It involves defining what is acceptable and unacceptable in your relationships and interactions. Boundaries help you maintain your sense of self and ensure that your needs and values are respected.

Try this: Reflect on areas in your life where boundaries are lacking or being violated. Practice asserting your needs and saying no when necessary. Remember, setting boundaries is an act of self-respect and a crucial part of reclaiming your identity.

Seek Support
The journey of self-discovery is deeply personal, but that doesn't mean you have to do it alone. Surround yourself with supportive people who respect and encourage your growth. This might include friends, family, therapists, or support groups.

Try this: Identify a few trusted individuals who you feel comfortable sharing your journey with. Communicate your goals and ask for their support and encouragement. Having a supportive network can provide motivation and reassurance as you navigate this path.

As you build this supportive network, it's also important to examine the narratives that have shaped you, particularly those handed down by your family. These narratives can be powerful forces that influence your identity, often in ways that don't reflect your true self.

Defining Oneself Outside of Family Narratives

Family narratives can be powerful forces that shape your identity, often in ways that don't reflect your true self. These narratives are the stories that families tell about who we are, how we should behave, and what we can achieve. They are often deeply ingrained, passed down through generations, and can subtly or overtly influence our beliefs and behaviors. While some family narratives can be supportive and empowering, others can be limiting and stifling, preventing us from fully embracing our authentic selves.

Growing up, you might have been told stories about your family's values, expectations, and roles. These stories might have dictated what was considered acceptable or unacceptable, what was praised or criticized, and what paths were deemed worthy or unworthy. Perhaps you were labeled as "the smart one," "the troublemaker," or "the caretaker." These labels can become self-fulfilling prophecies, shaping your choices and limiting your potential.

Consider the family that insists everyone must follow a certain career path to uphold a legacy, or the one that enforces strict gender roles, leaving little room for individuality. These narratives can be like invisible chains, holding you back from exploring and expressing who you truly are. They can create internal conflict, especially when your desires and aspirations don't align with the family's expectations.

Breaking free from these narratives involves a process of redefining who you are on your own terms. It requires introspection and courage to challenge the beliefs and expectations that have been imposed upon you. It's about questioning the stories you've been told and deciding which ones you want to keep, which ones you want to rewrite, and which ones you need to discard entirely.

This process can be daunting because it often involves stepping away from the comfort and familiarity of your family's expectations. It might mean facing resistance or disapproval from loved ones who are invested in maintaining the status quo. However, it's a crucial step towards reclaiming your identity and living a life that is true to yourself.

Think of this as an opportunity to become the author of your own life story. Instead of living out a script written by others, you get to write your own narrative, one that reflects your values, dreams, and aspirations. This journey is about finding your voice and using it to express who you are and what you stand for.

By redefining yourself outside of family narratives, you open up a world of possibilities. You give yourself permission to explore different aspects of your identity, to pursue passions that resonate with you, and to set goals that are meaningful to you. This is about embracing your uniqueness and celebrating the qualities that make you who you are.

Breaking free from family narratives is not about rejecting your family or their values entirely. It's about differentiating between what truly aligns with your authentic self and what doesn't. It's about creating a balanced perspective where you can honor your family's influence while also asserting your individuality.

Now, let's explore some practical steps to help you define yourself outside of family narratives:

Challenge Limiting Beliefs

Family narratives often come with limiting beliefs about who you are and what you can achieve. These beliefs can be deeply ingrained, but they are not immutable. Challenging and reframing these beliefs is a crucial step in reclaiming your identity.

Try this: Identify a limiting belief that you've inherited from your family. For example, "I'm not good enough" or "I must always put others first." Write it down and then challenge it by providing evidence to the contrary. Replace it with an empowering belief that reflects your true potential.

Create Your Own Story

Your life is your story to tell. Reclaiming your identity involves taking ownership of this narrative and writing it in a way that reflects your values, dreams, and aspirations. It's about becoming the author of your own life.

Try this: Write a short story or journal entry about your life from your perspective, focusing on your strengths, achievements, and aspirations. Use this narrative as a guiding light to help you make decisions and set goals that align with your true self.

Celebrate Your Uniqueness

Every person is unique, with their own blend of talents, quirks, and experiences. Embrace what makes you different and celebrate your individuality. This is not about fitting into a mold but about standing out and being authentically you.

Try this: Make a list of qualities and talents that make you unique. Reflect on how these traits have positively influenced your life and how you can leverage them to achieve your goals. Celebrate your individuality by doing something that makes you feel uniquely you, whether it's dressing in a way that expresses your personality or pursuing a hobby that you love.

Reclaiming your identity after trauma is a journey of self-discovery and empowerment. It's about peeling back the layers of shame and external expectations to reveal the true you. By reflecting on your values, exploring your passions, listening to your inner voice, setting boundaries, and seeking support, you can redefine yourself outside of family narratives and embrace your authentic self.

This journey is not about becoming someone new; it's about rediscovering and embracing who you've always been. You have the power to create a life that reflects your true self, filled with purpose, passion, and authenticity.

Keep moving forward, brave soul, and watch as you transform your life from the inside out.

CHAPTER 8
FOSTERING HEALTHY RELATIONSHIPS

Healthy relationships are the cornerstone of a fulfilling life. They provide us with support, love, and a sense of belonging. These connections can lift us up in times of need, offer a shoulder to lean on, and bring immense joy and satisfaction. But when you've experienced trauma and shame, building and maintaining these relationships can feel like navigating a minefield.

Trauma can leave you with deep-seated trust issues, making it hard to believe that others won't hurt you. You might find yourself constantly on guard, waiting for the other shoe to drop. The fear of vulnerability can be paralyzing, keeping you from opening up and forming genuine connections. You may have learned to build walls instead of bridges, isolating yourself in an attempt to protect your heart.

Setting boundaries can also be a significant challenge. Boundaries are essential for healthy relationships, but trauma and shame can distort your sense of what is acceptable. You might struggle to assert your needs, fearing rejection or conflict. Alternatively, you might have overly rigid boundaries, keeping everyone at a distance to avoid potential pain. Both extremes can prevent you from experiencing the deep, meaningful relationships that are vital for a fulfilling life.

But don't worry—this chapter will guide you through the process of building trust, forming healthy connections, and setting boundaries to protect your well-being. We'll explore practical strategies to help you navigate these challenges and create relationships that are supportive, loving, and grounded in mutual respect.

Imagine relationships as a garden. To thrive, they need attention, care, and the right conditions. Trust is the soil in which your connections grow, vulnerability is the water that nurtures them, and boundaries are the fences that protect them from harm. With the right balance, your relationships can flourish, providing you with the support and love you need to lead a fulfilling life.

Building Trust and Forming Healthy Connections

Trust is the foundation of any healthy relationship. Without it, relationships can feel unstable and insecure. Imagine building a house on a shaky foundation—it's only a matter of time before cracks appear and the structure begins to crumble. Similarly, without trust, even the most promising relationships can falter under the weight of doubt and suspicion.

Building trust is a gradual process, often requiring time, effort, and a willingness to be vulnerable. It's not about expecting perfection from yourself or others, but about consistently showing up with honesty and integrity.

Trust involves believing that others have your best interests at heart and that they will act with kindness and respect. It's about feeling safe enough to open up, share your true self, and rely on others for support.

For many people who have experienced trauma or shame, trusting others can be particularly challenging. Past experiences of betrayal or hurt can create barriers that make it difficult to believe in the goodwill of others. You might find yourself constantly questioning motives, fearing rejection, or waiting for the next shoe to drop. However, learning to trust again is an essential step towards forming healthy, fulfilling relationships.

Trust begins with small acts of faith—believing that a friend will keep a secret, that a partner will stay true, or that a family member will support you in times of need. These small acts build up over time, creating a solid foundation upon which deeper connections can be built. It's about giving and receiving the benefit of the doubt, understanding that everyone has their flaws and that trust is a two-way street.

In addition to time and effort, building trust requires vulnerability. Being vulnerable means allowing yourself to be seen and known, imperfections and all. It means taking the risk of being hurt, knowing that true connection is only possible when you are willing to open up. Vulnerability can be scary, but it is also incredibly powerful. It invites others to be vulnerable too, fostering mutual understanding and empathy.

Establishing trust also involves clear and open communication. It's about expressing your needs, boundaries, and expectations honestly and listening to others with an open heart. Misunderstandings and conflicts are inevitable in any relationship, but how you navigate these challenges can either strengthen or weaken the trust between you.

Trust is not a destination but a continuous journey. It requires ongoing commitment and care. Even in the strongest relationships, trust can be tested, but each test is an opportunity to deepen your connection and reaffirm your commitment to one another.

Here's how you can start fostering trust and forming healthy connections:

Be Authentic

Authenticity is key to building trust. When you are true to yourself, you invite others to do the same. This mutual honesty creates a solid foundation for trust.

Try this: Practice being open and honest about your thoughts, feelings, and experiences. Share your true self with others, even if it feels uncomfortable at first. Authenticity attracts authenticity, leading to deeper, more meaningful connections.

Communicate Effectively

Good communication is essential for healthy relationships. It involves not only expressing your own needs and feelings but also actively listening to others.

Try this: Practice active listening by giving your full attention to the person speaking, without interrupting or planning your response. Reflect back what you hear to ensure understanding. When expressing your own needs, use "I" statements (e.g., "I feel…" or "I need…") to avoid sounding accusatory.

By honing these communication skills, you lay the groundwork for deeper connections. This leads us to another crucial aspect of building trust and forming healthy relationships: fostering authenticity and effective communication.

Fostering Authenticity and Effective Communication

Authenticity and effective communication are the cornerstones of meaningful relationships. When you show up as your true self and communicate openly, you create a space where others feel safe to do the same. These elements are critical not only for building trust but also for fostering deep connections that are grounded in mutual respect and understanding.

Authenticity means being genuine and honest about who you are—your thoughts, feelings, strengths, and vulnerabilities. It involves letting go of the masks and personas we often wear to fit in or protect ourselves. When you are authentic, you allow others to see the real you, which can be both liberating and empowering. It's about embracing your true self, flaws and all, and inviting others to do the same.

Effective communication, on the other hand, is about how you convey your thoughts and feelings to others and how well you listen and understand what they communicate to you. It's not just about speaking clearly but also about listening actively and empathetically. Good communication involves a balance of expressing your own needs and validating the needs of others, creating a dialogue that fosters mutual understanding and respect.

When authenticity and effective communication come together, they create a powerful synergy that enhances the quality of your relationships. You feel more connected and understood, and you build stronger, more resilient bonds with the people in your life.

Here's why these elements are so crucial:

1. **Building Trust:** Authenticity and effective communication build trust by showing that you are reliable, honest, and open. When people see that you are being genuine, they are more likely to trust you and reciprocate with their own honesty and openness.

2. **Deepening Connections:** When you communicate authentically, you go beyond surface-level interactions and connect on a deeper level. Sharing your true self and listening to others with empathy and understanding creates a bond that is both meaningful and enduring.

3. **Resolving Conflicts:** Effective communication is key to resolving conflicts in a healthy way. By expressing your feelings honestly and listening to the other person's perspective, you can address issues constructively and find mutually agreeable solutions.

4. **Fostering Empathy:** Authenticity and good communication foster empathy by encouraging you to see things from others' perspectives. This mutual empathy strengthens your relationships by making you more attuned to each other's needs and experiences.

5. **Promoting Personal Growth:** Being authentic and communicating effectively promotes personal growth. It allows you to explore and express your true self, learn from others, and develop deeper self-awareness and emotional intelligence.

In practice, fostering authenticity and effective communication requires conscious effort and practice. It means being mindful of how you present yourself and how you interact with others. It involves taking risks, being vulnerable, and sometimes having difficult conversations.

But the rewards—deeper, more fulfilling relationships—are well worth the effort.

> Now, let's explore some practical steps to help you cultivate authenticity and effective communication in your relationships:

Be Genuine
Being genuine means showing up as you are, without pretense. It's about being honest about your thoughts, feelings, and experiences. When you're genuine, you create a space where others feel comfortable being themselves too.

Try this: Share something personal about your day, your thoughts, or your feelings with someone you trust. Notice how it feels to be open and how the other person responds. This openness can foster deeper connections and mutual understanding.

Listen Actively
Active listening is about truly hearing what the other person is saying, without planning your response or getting distracted. It involves giving your full attention and showing that you value their words.

Try this: When someone is speaking to you, focus entirely on what they're saying. Nod, maintain eye contact, and provide verbal affirmations like "I see" or "That makes sense." Reflect back what you've heard to ensure understanding and show that you're engaged.

Express Your Needs and Feelings

Clear communication about your needs and feelings helps prevent misunderstandings and builds trust. It's important to express yourself in a way that is respectful and constructive.

Try this: Use "I" statements to communicate your needs and feelings without blaming or criticizing. For example, say, "I feel overwhelmed and could use some support" instead of "You never help me." This approach fosters understanding and collaboration. Effective communication not only helps build trust and deepen connections but also lays the groundwork for another crucial aspect of healthy relationships: setting boundaries. Boundaries are essential for maintaining healthy relationships and protecting your mental and emotional health. They define what is acceptable and unacceptable behavior in your interactions with others.

Here's how to establish and maintain healthy boundaries:

Strategies for Setting Boundaries

Setting boundaries is essential for maintaining healthy relationships and protecting your mental and emotional health. Boundaries define what is acceptable and unacceptable behavior in your interactions with others. They act as guidelines that help you communicate your needs and protect your well-being. When you set clear boundaries, you create a safe space for yourself and others, fostering mutual respect and understanding.

Boundaries are not just about keeping others at a distance; they are about creating a balanced relationship where both parties feel valued and respected. They help prevent resentment and burnout by ensuring that your needs are met and that you are not constantly sacrificing your well-being for others. Healthy boundaries can lead to healthier, more fulfilling relationships where both individuals feel supported and understood.

Setting boundaries can be challenging, especially if you have been conditioned to put others' needs before your own or if you fear rejection or conflict. However, it is a vital skill for anyone looking to cultivate healthy relationships. Boundaries are not about being rigid or inflexible; they are about understanding your limits and communicating them effectively to others.

Imagine boundaries as the lines on a soccer field. They define the playing area and ensure that the game is fair and enjoyable for everyone involved. Without these lines, the game would be chaotic and confusing, with players constantly overstepping and clashing. Similarly, in relationships, boundaries help create a clear and respectful environment where everyone knows what to expect.

Establishing boundaries involves several key steps: identifying your boundaries, communicating them clearly, being assertive, enforcing them when necessary, and practicing self-care. Each of these steps is crucial for maintaining healthy relationships and protecting your emotional and mental health.

Here's how to establish and maintain healthy boundaries:

Identify Your Boundaries
The first step in setting boundaries is understanding what they are. Reflect on your needs, values, and limits to identify where you need to set boundaries.

Try this: Make a list of situations where you feel uncomfortable or stressed. Ask yourself what you need in these situations to feel safe and respected. These needs are the basis of your boundaries.

Communicate Your Boundaries Clearly
Once you've identified your boundaries, communicate them clearly to others. Use direct, respectful language to convey your needs.

Try this: Use "I" statements to communicate your boundaries without sounding accusatory. For example, "I need some time alone after work to unwind" or "I'm not comfortable discussing this topic."

Be Assertive
Setting boundaries requires assertiveness. It's important to stand firm in your boundaries, even when others push back.

Try this: Practice assertive communication by stating your boundaries clearly and confidently. Use a calm and steady tone, and maintain eye contact.

Remember, being assertive is not the same as being aggressive; it's about respecting yourself and others.

Enforce Your Boundaries
It's not enough to just set boundaries; you must also enforce them. This means taking action when your boundaries are crossed.

Try this: Decide in advance what the consequences will be if your boundaries are not respected. Communicate these consequences clearly and follow through if necessary. For example, "If you continue to raise your voice, I will leave the room."

Practice Self-Care
Setting boundaries is an act of self-care. It's about prioritizing your well-being and ensuring that your needs are met.

Try this: Make self-care a regular part of your routine. This might include activities like exercise, meditation, journaling, or spending time with loved ones. By taking care of yourself, you reinforce the importance of your boundaries and your right to have them respected. Self-care isn't just about pampering yourself; it's a vital part of maintaining your mental and emotional health. It reminds you that your needs matter and helps you recharge so you can be your best self in your relationships. When you prioritize self-care, you set a powerful example for others, demonstrating that respecting boundaries is crucial for mutual well-being.

Remember, boundaries are not walls meant to isolate you but bridges that create a healthy space for connection and growth. They allow you to engage with others from a place of strength and clarity, fostering relationships that are respectful and nurturing.

Building trust and forming healthy relationships after trauma and shame is a challenging but essential part of the healing journey. By being authentic, communicating effectively, showing consistency, being vulnerable, and respecting boundaries, you can foster deep and meaningful connections. Setting and enforcing boundaries is crucial for maintaining these relationships and protecting your mental and emotional health.

As you embark on this journey, remember that progress is a series of small steps. Celebrate your victories, no matter how minor they seem, and be gentle with yourself when you stumble. Each effort you make to build trust, communicate openly, and set boundaries is a testament to your courage and commitment to a healthier, more fulfilling life.

Healthy relationships are built on mutual respect, trust, and understanding. As you continue to heal and grow, you'll find that the connections you form are not only stronger but also more fulfilling. Keep moving forward, brave soul, and embrace the power of healthy relationships in your life. You deserve relationships that uplift and support you, and with these tools, you're well on your way to creating them.

CHAPTER 9
BREAKING THE CYCLE

Breaking the cycle of toxic shame is one of the most important and impactful things you can do, especially if you are a parent or plan to be one. The patterns of behavior and beliefs that we inherit from our families can be powerful, but they are not unchangeable. With conscious effort and intentionality, you can create a healthier environment for your children, free from the toxic shame that may have plagued your own upbringing.

Imagine the legacy you can leave: a legacy of resilience, self-worth, and unconditional love. It's about rewriting the script that has been handed down through generations, transforming it into one that fosters growth and positive self-image. This isn't just about preventing harm; it's about actively nurturing and uplifting your children, giving them the tools they need to thrive.

The process of breaking this cycle begins with awareness. Recognizing the toxic patterns and beliefs that were instilled in you allows you to consciously choose a different path. It requires a commitment to self-reflection and a willingness to confront uncomfortable truths about your own experiences and behaviors. By understanding the origins of your own shame, you can prevent it from seeping into your parenting.

Think of it as being an emotional archeologist, digging through the layers of your past to uncover the sources of shame and examining them with compassion and understanding. This process is not about blame; it's about empowerment. By identifying the harmful patterns, you gain the power to change them and to create a new, healthier narrative for your family.

Conscious effort means being deliberate in your actions and choices as a parent. It involves setting clear intentions about the kind of environment you want to create for your children. This might include fostering open communication, where feelings and thoughts can be expressed without fear of judgment or shame. It also means modeling healthy behavior, demonstrating how to handle mistakes with grace and how to treat oneself and others with kindness and respect.

Intentionality in parenting is about making thoughtful decisions that prioritize the emotional well-being of your children. It's about being present and engaged, listening to their needs, and responding with empathy. This intentional approach helps to build a foundation of trust and security, where children feel safe to be themselves and explore their identities without the burden of toxic shame.

Creating a shame-free environment doesn't mean that challenges and conflicts won't arise. They will, as they do in all families. However, the way you respond to these challenges makes all the difference. Instead of resorting to criticism or punishment, focus on constructive feedback and support. Encourage a growth mindset, where mistakes are seen as opportunities for learning rather than as evidence of inadequacy.

Breaking the cycle of toxic shame is a journey, not a destination. It requires continuous effort and a commitment to personal growth. There will be setbacks and moments of self-doubt, but each step forward is a victory. By making these changes, you are not only improving your children's lives but also healing your own wounds. You are creating a new legacy, one where shame is replaced with love, acceptance, and empowerment.

The impact of breaking this cycle extends beyond your immediate family. It influences how your children will interact with the world and how they will raise their own children in the future. By fostering a healthy environment, you are contributing to a more compassionate and understanding society, one generation at a time.

Guidance for Parents or Future Parents

Parenting is one of the most challenging and rewarding jobs you can undertake. It's a role that requires patience, love, and a commitment to growth—not just for your children, but for yourself as well. Being a parent means constantly learning and adapting, as each child is unique and each stage of their development presents new challenges and opportunities.

The journey of parenting is like navigating uncharted waters. There will be storms and calm seas, and sometimes you might feel lost. But with patience and a clear sense of direction, you can guide your children towards safe harbors. It's about being present and engaged, understanding that your actions and words have a profound impact on their development.

Patience is key because children are learning how to navigate the world and their emotions. They will test boundaries and make mistakes as they figure out who they are and how they fit into the world. Your ability to remain calm and patient, even in the face of frustration, teaches them that it's okay to make mistakes and that they are loved regardless.

Love is the foundation of all healthy parenting. It's not just about the affection you show, but also about creating an environment where your children feel secure, valued, and understood. Love is about being there for them, listening to their needs, and providing a safe space for them to grow and explore their identities.

A commitment to growth means recognizing that parenting is a continuous learning process. Just as you are guiding your children through their development, you too are growing and evolving. This involves being open to new ideas, seeking out resources and support, and reflecting on your parenting practices. It's about being willing to make changes and improvements to better support your children's needs.

As a parent, you set the tone for your children's emotional and psychological development. The way you handle your own emotions and challenges serves as a model for them. By showing them how to navigate life's ups and downs with resilience and compassion, you provide them with a valuable blueprint for their own lives.

Mindful parenting is about being aware of your actions and their impact on your children. It's about being present in the moment, truly listening to your children, and responding to their needs with empathy and understanding. Mindfulness in parenting helps you stay connected with your children and fosters a deeper bond based on mutual respect and trust.

Nurturing your children involves more than just meeting their physical needs. It's about supporting their emotional, social, and intellectual development. This means encouraging their curiosity, celebrating their achievements, and helping them develop a positive sense of self. It's about providing guidance and boundaries while also allowing them the freedom to grow and explore.

Parenting is not about being perfect; it's about being present and willing to grow alongside your children. It's about learning from your mistakes and striving to do better each day. By approaching parenting with patience, love, and a commitment to growth, you can create a supportive and nurturing environment for your children.

Here are some strategies to help you become a more mindful and nurturing parent:

Reflect on Your Own Upbringing
Understanding your own experiences with shame can help you avoid repeating those patterns with your children. Reflect on the messages you received

growing up and consider how they have impacted you.

Try this: Write down specific instances where you felt shamed as a child. Reflect on how these experiences affected your self-esteem and behavior. This awareness can help you identify triggers and patterns that you want to avoid passing on to your children.

Practice Self-Compassion
Modeling self-compassion is crucial for teaching your children to be kind to themselves. When you make mistakes, show your children that it's okay to be imperfect and that learning and growth come from these experiences.

Try this: The next time you make a mistake, talk about it openly with your children. Explain what you learned and how you will try to do better next time. This shows them that everyone makes mistakes and that self compassion is key to overcoming them.

Communicate Openly and Honestly
Open and honest communication builds trust and helps your children feel safe and understood. Encourage them to express their feelings and listen to them without judgment.

Try this: Set aside regular time to talk with your children about their day, their feelings, and any concerns they might have. Make it a habit to validate their feelings and provide reassurance, showing that their emotions are important and worthy of attention.

Set Healthy Boundaries
Boundaries are essential for a healthy parent-child relationship. They provide structure and safety, but it's important that they are clear, consistent, and respectful.

Try this: Establish family rules and expectations together. Involve your children in the process so they understand the reasons behind the boundaries and feel a sense of ownership and respect for them.

Encourage Independence
Supporting your children's independence helps them develop confidence and a sense of self-worth. Allow them to make choices and take responsibility for their actions in age-appropriate ways.

Try this: Give your children opportunities to make decisions about their daily activities, such as choosing their clothes or deciding on a weekend activity. This fosters their decision-making skills and helps them feel empowered.

By encouraging independence and fostering decision-making skills, you lay a foundation for your children to develop confidence and self-worth. But empowering your children is just one piece of the puzzle. To truly break the cycle of toxic shame, it's crucial to create an environment where they feel valued, accepted, and loved for who they are.

Avoiding Toxic Shame in the Next Generation

Breaking the cycle of toxic shame means creating an environment where your children feel valued, accepted, and loved for who they are. Think of yourself as the Gandalf of your family, standing firm and declaring, "You shall not pass!" to the toxic shame that's tried to infiltrate your lineage. It's about rewriting the script from "Game of Thrones" levels of family dysfunction to something more like "The Wonder Years"—full of growth, understanding, and a dash of nostalgia.

Creating this shame-free zone isn't just about removing negative influences; it's about actively promoting positive ones. It's about showing your kids that they are more than their mistakes, that their worth isn't tied to their achievements, and that they have the freedom to be themselves—quirks, flaws, and all. This might mean challenging some deep-seated family traditions, but hey, someone's got to break the cycle, right?

You're not just parenting; you're on a mission to dismantle the emotional landmines and build a sanctuary of self-worth and acceptance.

Here's how you can channel your inner superhero and ensure your kids grow up feeling like the amazing, unique individuals they are:

Affirm Their Worth
Regularly affirm your children's worth and value, regardless of their achievements or behavior. Let them know that they are loved unconditionally.

Try this: Make a habit of telling your children that you love them and are proud of them, not just for what they do, but for who they are. Praise their efforts and qualities, not just their accomplishments.

Avoid Comparisons
Comparing your children to others can foster feelings of inadequacy and shame. Celebrate their unique strengths and talents instead.

Try this: Focus on your children's individual progress and achievements. Avoid statements like, "Why can't you be more like your sibling?" and instead highlight their personal growth and efforts.

Teach Emotional Regulation
Helping your children understand and manage their emotions can prevent feelings of shame. Teach them that all emotions are valid and provide tools for coping with difficult feelings.

Try this: Use tools like emotion charts or mindfulness exercises to help your children identify and express their emotions. Practice deep breathing or other calming techniques together during moments of stress.

Be Mindful of Your Words
The language you use can either build up or tear down your children's self-esteem. Choose words that are supportive and constructive.

Try this: Replace negative or critical language with positive reinforcement. Instead of saying, "You always mess up," try, "Let's see how we can improve this together."

Create a Safe Space for Failure
Allowing your children to fail and learn from their mistakes without fear of shame is crucial for their development. Encourage them to take risks and view failures as opportunities for growth.

Try this: Celebrate your children's efforts, even when the outcome isn't perfect. Discuss what they learned from the experience and how they can apply that knowledge in the future.

Breaking the cycle of toxic shame is a transformative process that not only heals your own wounds but also creates a healthier, more nurturing environment for your children. By reflecting on your own upbringing, practicing self-compassion, communicating openly, setting healthy boundaries, and encouraging independence, you can foster a positive and supportive atmosphere.

Remember, parenting is a journey filled with learning and growth. As you work towards breaking the cycle, you're not only benefiting your children but also future generations. Keep moving forward, brave soul, and embrace the power of positive, shame-free parenting. Your efforts are planting seeds of self-worth, resilience, and love that will flourish for years to come.

So, keep moving forward, brave soul. Embrace the power of positive, shame-free parenting. Each step you take in this journey is a step toward a legacy of strength and compassion. Your efforts are not just shaping your children's lives; they are building a future where kindness and acceptance are the norm. Stand tall in your mission, knowing that you are making an indelible impact that will resonate far beyond your own family.

CHAPTER 10
PRACTICAL EXERCISES & RESOURCES

As you journey through the process of healing and breaking the cycle of toxic shame, having practical tools and resources at your disposal can be incredibly beneficial. This emotional toolkit is filled with everything you need to navigate the rocky terrain of personal growth. This chapter is designed to provide you with hands-on activities, journaling prompts, guided meditations, and a list of additional resources to support your continued growth and healing.

These exercises and resources are like the Swiss Army knife of emotional resilience—versatile, practical, and indispensable. Whether you're a seasoned journaling pro or new to the idea of mindfulness, there's something here for everyone. By incorporating these practices into your daily life, you can create a foundation of self-awareness, self-compassion, and emotional strength.

Imagine yourself as the protagonist in an epic adventure, armed with the knowledge and tools to conquer the dragons of shame and self-doubt. Each journaling prompt, meditation, and activity is a stepping stone on your path to self-discovery and empowerment. They are designed to help you peel back the layers of negative conditioning, challenge harmful beliefs, and cultivate a more positive and compassionate relationship with yourself.

Think of these exercises as your personal training montage, like Rocky preparing for the big fight or Mulan gearing up to save China. They might not involve punching meat slabs or climbing poles with buckets of water, but they are just as crucial for building your inner strength and resilience. By engaging with these tools regularly, you're training your mind and heart to embrace healing and reject the toxic shame that has held you back.

This chapter is not just about giving you tasks to check off a list. It's about inviting you to create a daily practice that fosters growth and transformation. It's about carving out time for yourself amidst the chaos of life, to pause, reflect, and nurture your soul. Whether you have five minutes or an hour, these exercises can be tailored to fit your schedule and meet you where you are.

The goal is to make healing a part of your everyday life, not just something you do in therapy sessions or during crises. It's about creating a sustainable, ongoing process of self-care and self-improvement. Each tool and resource in this chapter is a reminder that you have the power to change your narrative, to build a life free from the shadows of shame, and to step into your true, unburdened self.

So, let's dive in and explore these practical exercises and resources. They are your allies in this journey, ready to support you every step of the way. Remember, healing is not a destination but a journey. With these tools, you can navigate the twists and turns with confidence, knowing that each step forward, no matter how small, is a victory.

Journaling Prompts

Journaling is a powerful tool for self-reflection and personal growth. It allows you to explore your thoughts and feelings in a safe, private space, helping you to gain clarity and understanding. Think of journaling as having a conversation with your most honest and insightful friend—yourself. It's a space where you can be completely open and unfiltered, where no thought or feeling is too big, too small, or too messy to be acknowledged.

By putting pen to paper, you create a tangible record of your inner world. This act of writing can help you process complex emotions, identify patterns in your thoughts and behaviors, and uncover insights that might not be apparent in the hustle and bustle of daily life. Journaling can be both a mirror and a window: a mirror that reflects your true self back to you and a window that opens up new perspectives and possibilities.

Moreover, journaling is a therapeutic practice that can reduce stress, enhance your mood, and provide a sense of control over your life. It's a tool for grounding yourself in the present moment, for sorting through the clutter of your mind, and for making sense of the experiences that shape you. Whether you're grappling with the remnants of toxic shame, navigating a current challenge, or simply seeking to understand yourself better, journaling can be a valuable ally.

Here are some journaling prompts to help you delve deeper into your experiences and emotions. Each prompt is designed to guide you toward greater self-awareness and healing, providing a structured way to explore the depths of your psyche. Don't worry about writing perfectly or censoring yourself—just let your thoughts flow freely and see where the journey takes you.

1. Reflect on Your Childhood: Write about a specific memory from your childhood that impacted your sense of self-worth. How did it make you feel then, and how does it affect you now?

2. Identify Shame Triggers: List the situations or interactions that trigger feelings of shame for you. What thoughts and emotions arise in these moments?

3. Reframe Negative Beliefs: Identify a negative belief you hold about yourself. Challenge this belief by writing down evidence that contradicts it and reframing it into a positive affirmation.

4. Celebrate Your Strengths: Write about your strengths and accomplishments. How have these qualities helped you overcome challenges in your life?

5. Set Boundaries: Reflect on a time when you felt your boundaries were respected or violated. How did it make you feel, and what can you do to ensure your boundaries are upheld in the future?

6. Practice Self-Compassion: Write a letter to yourself expressing kindness and understanding for a mistake or difficult situation you've faced. What would you say to a friend in a similar situation?

Guided Meditations

Meditation can be a powerful practice for calming the mind, reducing stress, and cultivating a sense of inner peace. In our fast-paced world, taking a few moments to center yourself can make all the difference in how you handle life's challenges. Guided meditations, in particular, can offer structure and support as you embark on or deepen your mindfulness practice. Think of them as your personal guide through the labyrinth of your mind, helping you navigate to a place of calm and clarity.

Meditation isn't just about sitting in silence; it's about creating a mental space where you can breathe freely, let go of stress, and connect with your inner self. Whether you're a seasoned meditator or a complete beginner, guided meditations can help you focus, providing gentle prompts that keep your mind from wandering. These meditations can be tailored to address specific needs, such as releasing stress, fostering self-compassion, or cultivating gratitude.

Here are some guided meditations to support your healing journey. Each one is designed to address different aspects of your emotional well-being, providing you with tools to enhance your mental and emotional health.

1. Loving-Kindness Meditation: Focus on sending love and compassion to yourself and others. Repeat phrases like, "May I be happy, may I be healthy, may I be safe, may I live with ease."

2. Body Scan Meditation: Bring awareness to different parts of your body, releasing tension and fostering a sense of connection to your physical self.

3. Visualization Meditation: Imagine a place where you feel completely safe and at peace. Visualize the details of this place and allow yourself to fully experience the sense of calm it brings.

4. Breath Awareness Meditation: Focus on your breath, observing the sensation of each inhale and exhale. Use your breath as an anchor to stay present and grounded.

5. Gratitude Meditation: Reflect on the things you are grateful for. Allow feelings of gratitude to fill your heart and mind, cultivating a positive outlook.

Hands-On Activities

Engaging in creative and physical activities can also support your healing process. These activities provide a tangible way to express and process your emotions, connect with your body, and find joy and relaxation. Think of them as the hands-on component of your emotional toolbox—practices that not only help you cope but also encourage growth, creativity, and resilience. Whether you're painting your feelings onto a canvas, stretching out tension through yoga, or finding solace in nature, these activities can be powerful allies in your healing journey.

Hands-on activities offer a break from the constant whirl of thoughts, allowing you to engage with the present moment and focus on the here and now. They can help you develop a deeper connection with yourself and the world around you, fostering a sense of accomplishment and satisfaction.

Here are some hands-on activities to try, each designed to support your mental, emotional, and physical well-being:

1. Art Therapy: Use drawing, painting, or sculpting to express your emotions and experiences. There's no need to focus on the outcome—just let your creativity flow.

2. Mindful Movement: Practice yoga, tai chi, or simple stretching exercises to connect with your body and release tension.

3. Nature Walks: Spend time in nature, observing the sights, sounds, and smells around you. Allow yourself to feel grounded and connected to the natural world.

4. Affirmation Cards: Create a set of affirmation cards with positive statements about yourself. Pull a card each day for inspiration and encouragement.

5. Gratitude Jar: Write down things you are grateful for on slips of paper and place them in a jar. When you're feeling down, read through the notes to remind yourself of the positive aspects of your life.

Additional Resources

Continued healing and growth often require ongoing support and resources. The journey to overcoming toxic shame and fostering self-compassion is a lifelong process, and having access to additional tools and guidance can make all the difference. Just as a hero in an epic quest needs allies and wisdom to face challenges, you too can benefit from the knowledge and support offered by various books, websites, and organizations. These resources can provide you with new perspectives, practical advice, and a sense of community as you navigate your healing journey.

Whether you're looking for deeper insights into your experiences, practical strategies for daily living, or professional support, these resources are here to help. Think of them as your personal library of wisdom and support, available whenever you need a helping hand or a dose of inspiration.

Here are some recommended books, websites, and organizations to further support your journey:

Books

- "**The Gifts of Imperfection**" by Brené Brown
- "**Self-Compassion: The Proven Power of Being Kind to Yourself**" by Kristin Neff
- "**Healing the Shame That Binds You**" by John Bradshaw
- "**The Body Keeps the Score**" by Bessel van der Kolk

Websites

- **Mindful.org**: Resources for mindfulness and meditation practices.
- **Self-Compassion.org**: Guided meditations and exercises by Kristin Neff.
- **The Gottman Institute**: Resources for building healthy relationships.

Organizations

- **National Alliance on Mental Illness (NAMI)**: Support and resources for mental health.
- **Mental Health America (MHA)**: Information and resources for mental wellness.
- **Psychology Today**: Directory of therapists and articles on mental health topics.

As you continue on your journey of healing and self-discovery, remember that progress is not always linear. Sometimes it's two steps forward, one step back, and occasionally a faceplant into the mud. But hey, that's life, right? Each stumble, fall, and victory brings you closer to a healthier, more fulfilling life. Use these practical exercises and resources to support your growth, and know that you are not alone. You've got this, and there's a whole squad of us cheering you on.

Your commitment to breaking the cycle of toxic shame and fostering a positive, nurturing environment for yourself and your loved ones is a powerful testament to your strength and resilience. Think of yourself as the superhero of your own story—no capes necessary, just a heart full of courage and a mind ready to kick some toxic shame to the curb. Keep moving forward, brave soul. The path ahead is filled with opportunities for healing, growth, and profound transformation.

But don't think this is the end of our journey together. This is just the beginning. We'll catch up soon with more on navigating the wild ride of life, diving deeper into self-compassion, resilience, and whatever else the universe throws our way. So, keep shining, keep fighting, and don't forget to laugh at the absurdities along the way. Your story is just getting started, and it's going to be epic.

REFERENCES

Books:

Brown, B. (2010).
The Gifts of Imperfection: Let Go of Who You Think You're Supposed to Be and Embrace Who You Are.
Hazelden Publishing.

Kaufman, G. (1992).
Shame: The Power of Caring.
Schenkman Books.

Walker, P. (2013).
Complex PTSD: From Surviving to Thriving: A Guide and Map for Recovering from Childhood Trauma.
CreateSpace Independent Publishing Platform.

Bradshaw, J. (2005).
Healing the Shame that Binds You.
Health Communications Inc.

Gibson, L.C. (2015).
Adult Children of Emotionally Immature Parents: How to Heal from Distant, Rejecting, or Self-Involved Parents.
New Harbinger Publications.

Articles:

Herman, J. L. (1992).
Complex PTSD: A syndrome in survivors of prolonged and repeated trauma.
Journal of Traumatic Stress, 5(3), 377-391.

Levine, P. A. (1997).
Waking the Tiger: Healing Trauma.
North Atlantic Books.

Smith, M., Robinson, L., & Segal, J (2022).
Dealing with a Toxic Family or Parents: Recognizing, Handling, and Avoiding Unhealthy Relationships.
HelpGuide.org.

Parker, K. (2021).
The Lifelong Effects of Toxic Parenting and How to Break the Cycle.
Psych Central

Brown, B. (2006).
Shame Resiliece Theory: A Grounded Theory Study on Women and Shame.
Families in Society: The Journal of Contemporary Social Services, 87(1), 43-52.

Websites:

Mindful.
http://www.mindful.org.

Psych Central.
http://www.psychcentral.com.

RAINN.
RAINN.org: Rape, Abuse & Incest National Network.
http://www.rainn.org.

Talkspace.
Talkspace: Online Therapy with Licensed Therapists.
http://www.talkspace.com.

The Mighty.
The Mighty: a digital health community.
http://www.themighty.com.

ABOUT THE AUTHOR

Meet S.Y. Vidal, an artist at heart who thrives on creativity. Whether drawing, painting, writing, or diving into the psychological thrills of a horror movie, Vidal lives for artistic expression. Oh, and let's not forget the cats—each one is a muse and practically part of the writing team.

   While Vidal's degree might not be in psychology, it still hangs proudly next to his priceless artwork—both testaments to the school of life. Let's say his wisdom comes less from textbooks and more from a curriculum set by a harsh yet enlightening life journey. It's the advice you'd get from a friend who may not know Pi to the 20th decimal but knows how to piece together a broken soul. Vidal writes how he talks—no holds barred, heartfelt, and relatable. The aim? To dive deep but keep it real, just like a chat with an old friend who's seen it all.

   When the pen is down, and the paints are packed away, Vidal immerses himself in the rich landscapes and vibrant culture of Puerto Rico. The island's natural beauty is not just a backdrop but a source of endless inspiration. Ultimately, Vidal stands by the mantra that the only person who can truly save you is yourself. It's a belief that anchors him and acts as the cornerstone of his work. Through his books, art, and voice, he empowers others to dig deep and discover their hidden wellsprings of strength.

YOUR VOICE MATTERS

If this book has been a companion on your healing journey, if it's helped you understand, process, or begin to heal from childhood trauma, I would be deeply grateful if you would take a moment to share your experience.

Your review isn't just words on a page—it's a beacon of hope for others who might be struggling, feeling alone, or searching for understanding. By sharing how this book touched your life, you could be the lifeline someone else needs to take their first step towards healing.

Would you consider leaving a review on:

- Amazon
- Goodreads
- Google Books

Every review, every shared story, has the power to make a difference. Thank you for being brave, for your journey, and for potentially helping another soul find their path to healing.

With gratitude & hope,

ALSO AVAILABLE

WHO NEEDS SANTA
SHADOWS OF SHAME: OVERCOMING TOXIC SHAMING AND EMBRACING SELF-WORTH
S.Y. VIDAL

WHO NEEDS SANTA
& OTHER LESSONS IN SURVIVING TOXIC PARENTS
S.Y. VIDAL

SCOTTIE & THE HARE
FROM THE SERIES "SCOTTIE & THE WORLD"
A CHILDREN'S STORY • WRITTEN & ILLUSTRATED BY S.Y. VIDAL

LIFE'S A MESS AND THEN YOU TURN 40
LESSONS IN GROWTH AND RESILIENCE
S.Y. VIDAL

Signed Copies Available @
www.syvidalbooks.com

www.ingramcontent.com/pod-product-compliance
Lightning Source LLC
Chambersburg PA
CBHW071123090426
42736CB00012B/1997